Falling Hard for Fifty

A.C. ROSE

Falling Hard for Fifty
Goddess Communications
Copyright © 2015 by A.C. Rose

Cover Design: Najla Qamber Designs
Proofreading: Marla S. Esposito at Proofing with Style
Formatting: Polgarus Studio

This is meant to be a transformative work in that it adds or extends the existing knowledge base. The author utilized APA style attribution of quotations and concepts. APA format uses author-date method of in-text citation. This means that the author's last name and the year of publication for the source should appear in the text, for example, (Jones, 1998), and a complete reference should appear in the reference list at the end of the paper. We have followed that style.

Expert interviews appeared in existing articles by this author and fan interviews were gathered over many occasions and used by permission.

Dedication

This book is for fans of *Fifty Shades of Grey,*
the ones who fell in love with the story,
the characters and their world.

Gratitude to E.L. James,
for giving us the love story between Christian and Ana,
and igniting all our senses along the way.

And to the authors who stepped up to
write more good steamy love stories.

Contents

Introduction:

Captivated by Christian Grey—Me Included!

I never planned on reading *Fifty Shades of Grey*.

As it happened, I was editor of a love and sex web magazine at the time it took the world by storm and my boss told me *I had to read it* and create content and articles related to Christian Grey *because everyone was talking about him*!

As a former editor of *Playgirl* magazine and an author of steamy books in the nineties, I kind of assumed I had been there, done that. But I forced myself through the first few pages of book one, and then, it took me over. Oh yeah, it hooked me ... and I could not put it down. Over six days I worked my way through the trilogy, taking long lunches and reading during every moment of free time. When it was over I had what I now can identify as an unbelievable "book hangover."

I was literally in some sort of stupor, lost in the world of Christian Grey and Anastasia Steele. And I did not want to come out!

Bereft, I started looking around the Internet and Facebook and found hundreds, then thousands, of women who were feeling just the same. They were all in a deep state of yearning — stirred up by the story — and many appeared to be somewhat addicted to Christian Grey. Phrases such as "Laters, Baby," "We aim to please," and "Oh my" became part of our common vernacular. Many of us found ourselves constantly biting our lips. And the word "Greysessed" was showing up all over the Internet and it was something we all seemed to understand. The books had given us a common language and experience.

Like other fans, I began to "get over" the shock of the story ending by musing about my major crush on Christian Grey, talking about the trilogy, and searching for new books to read. It was hard to find anything that compared to that reading experience of *Fifty* so I dove into online communities that obsessed about the series, and that posted photos of hot men they imagined could be Christian Grey in the movie version. This was the kind of "fan casting" that went on way before many of us knew who Jamie Dornan was, a time when we could indulge completely in our individual fantasies of men who most captured the physical essence of the Christian that existed in the theater of our minds.

In fact, because of the deep fan interest in imagining what Mr. Grey might look like in real life, I produced an online photo slideshow of a dozen actors who might portray him and it got fifteen million page views — and a hundred comments from fans agreeing or not agreeing with the choices. It was more than a pastime or sport. Fans had serious opinions on this topic.

Just after reading the trilogy, I discovered author E.L. James was on a book tour in New York and that she would be at Barnes and Noble on 17th Street in Manhattan on May 15, 2012. Excited, I raced over and stood on line with a hundred people — four hundred had already moved through — to meet the woman who created it all. She was attractive, and seemed very lovely and normal! She did not have a twitchy palm, but her hand was hurting from so many autographs. Regardless, she carried on and signed my book, "*Laters, Baby.*" I felt like I had met royalty.

I took the opportunity to introduce myself as a journalist to the author and her publicist and asked if I might interview her when the dust settled on the book tour. They both agreed. But the dust never did settle and the trilogy took off like a rocket ship. I never got my interview—or the chance to ask her directly, back then, why she thought her sexy, gorgeous, damaged dominant had gotten so deeply under our skin.

But the curious journalist and relationship editor in me wanted to know: *What happened to us? What is it that touched such a deep longing in readers? What is the secret sauce or the magic ingredient that made so many of us go gaga for Mr. Grey? What was it about that book that made us fall so hard?*

As of this writing, I have been on the *Fifty Shades of Grey* beat for over three years, searching for those answers and reveling—with so many other authors and fans—in the new erotic romance revolution brought about by Ms. James.

In addition to covering the fun burst of erotic expression women experience reading it, I've been researching and reporting on the psychological, sociological, and sexual aspects of what led millions of women to fall in love with the story and characters, especially with Mr. Christian Grey.

I started the *Fifty Shades of Grey News* fan page on Facebook originally to gather insights from fans, and continue it as a labor of love. I have interacted with thousands of fans over the years, in addition to interviewing dozens of experts on this topic.

Coincidentally, while covering this story, I returned to college for a psychology degree. I was so taken with the *Fifty Shades of Grey* phenomenon that I convinced my professor to let me write about it for my final paper in a course called "Theories in Love and Romance." And I got an A!

Because I know there are so many fans, like me, who fell under the spell of *Fifty Shades*, I decided to turn my college paper, and the stories I researched and wrote in the years that followed, into an eBook and publish it for others to enjoy.

The Goals of My Initial Research

My aim was to try to discover how the *Fifty Shades of Grey* trilogy and Christian Grey stole our hearts. Clearly there was something that compelled millions of us to sign up for the rollercoaster of love and sex! I was curious if there was a way to "unpack it," and discover how specific aspects of the story may have touched readers. So I began to look at human attraction, desire, and love through the fictional characters Christian Grey and Anastasia (Ana) Steele—their story, their experience, and their love. I was curious about some of the following points:

- What can readers learn about love and romance from the perspective of brain science and love chemistry
- Why do Ana and Christian's experiences in *Fifty Shades of Grey* seem so real to fans and what makes the story come alive in the theater of the mind?
- What made so many readers fall in love with these characters, and their story, and what is happening in the reader's mind and body as they move through the story with these characters?
- Since there was such a controversy over who would play Christian Grey in the movie version of *Fifty Shades*, I wanted to also understand why fans get so attached to fictional characters, as well as their vision of the character's physical appearance.

While Christian and Anastasia are, of course, fictional, the progression of their love, the feelings they express, and the sexual experiences they have do seem real to readers. It seemed to me like we were right there with them – in Charlie Tango, in the Red Room, at the breakfast bar, on the piano, on the boat, etc. You could almost feel your wrists burn when Christian adjusted that gray tie and looked over at Ana during the graduation speech. *Right?*

When I started this research, the trilogy had recently been released by Vintage Books, an imprint of Random House (now Penguin Random House). Random House had snatched it up from the small Australian publisher, The Writer's Coffee Shop, which launched E.L. James after an earlier version of the work, *Master of the Universe*, had gone viral in the online world of fanfiction. The world was on fire with Christian Grey mania. The *Fifty Shades of Grey* movie had been optioned by Universal Studios, and fans were going mad lobbying for their favorite actors. Then there was a period of delays in casting and production that put the *Fifty Shades* fan world into turmoil. After much ado about every detail of getting the film launched, and ongoing pressure from fans to make sure it represented the book perfectly, the movie was *finally* released. It broke records around the world—over five million dollars at the box office — and producers are at work on *Fifty Shades Darker and Fifty Shades Freed.*

When I first told my college professor I wanted to do a final paper on Christian Grey, she had never heard of him. Since then there have been studies and college courses on the book and the characters. Much has happened since the *Fifty Shades of Grey* trilogy rocked our world and launched erotic romances, BDSM, and kinky love stories into the mainstream.

The books have also been highly controversial and have come under the fire of critics. People have complained about the quality of the writing in *Fifty Shades of Grey*, but I would argue that E.L. James was masterful in her use of erotic cues, and storytelling that stimulates all the senses. Personally, I am a huge fan of hers for opening the door to a brave new world where women of all ages can enjoy reading — and writing — erotic romances without shame. It's about time, right?

In this book I attempt to take a deeper look at this amazing publishing phenomenon and how it has become such a personal experience for so many readers. For proper academic attribution, I left the APA (American Psychological Association) style references in the chapters related research because I included quotes and concepts from the works of many others and also quote from the work of Ms. James. My college paper-turned-eBook, and additional reportage, is not affiliated or endorsed by E.L. James or her publisher. I do hope this is received as homage and tribute, as it is created with that intention.

As it would turn out, on June 18, 2015 I had a chance to meet E.L. James, again, at a birthday party for Christian Grey on Long Island to launch her new book, *Grey*.

In a few small sentences she gave me her answer to the question I'd been researching all this time: **Why did women fall so hard for Christian Grey?**

I share that on the final pages of the book.

—A.C. Rose

Part One

The Sexy Love Story that Changed Everything

Chapter 1

Fifty Shades Changed Publishing … And Readers

Fifty Shades of Grey was my first experience with this kind of fandom and perhaps this is one of the reasons it touched me so deeply. It also got me reading fiction again! Clearly, though, I am in good company.

Over 100 million books have been sold and all three books were on the *New York Times* Best Seller list for a long run—over one hundred weeks. The movie put them back on top. While the trilogy follows a romantic fiction formula spiced with eroticism and suspense, it somehow captured reader's attention like no other book of its kind. *Fifty Shades* kicked open an exciting new door in publishing and it inspired many imitations since; and many new and wonderful books and authors have cropped up in the erotic romance landscape.

It is safe to say *Fifty Shades of Grey* is responsible for opening a new conversation about female sexuality and, frankly, can be credited with taking the lid off when it comes to public discourse on all things sexual. It also appears to have inspired a new appreciation of the shirtless male and as well the public, online ogling of hot men.

According to sex therapists, psychologists, and fans, the books and related phenomenon have helped restore passion to relationships and encouraged people to experiment. On her web site, E.L. James calls her genre "Provocative Romance." Indeed it is.

Although some of the fans that flocked to *Fifty Shades of Grey* were an outflow from the phenomenally successful *Twilight* book and movie series (because it admittedly began as *Twilight* fanfiction), *Fifty Shades* stirred up its own intensity and interest in many new readers who had never witnessed nor have been part of a literary and social phenomenon like the explosion of *Fifty Shades of Grey* into the publishing world and out into the world at large.

While other generations have had their fan favorites and taboo love stories – *Gone with the Wind, The Thorn Birds,* and, of course, *Twilight* – this appears to be the first time in the modern era that we have seen a book create such a worldwide conversation about sexuality, and specifically, about kinky sex. With the *Fifty Shades* movement came a surge in acceptance of erotic romantic fiction, as well as an outward expression of female sexual desire (unlike anything we've seen since the sexual revolution, to my mind).

Kathryn Falk has kept our imaginations alive for decades presenting sexy cover models in her *Romantic Times Magazine* and Romantic Times Booklovers Conventions. We've seen the ogling of men on shows like *Ally McBeal* and were treated to the romantic and sexual adventures of single gals in *Sex and the City,* but *Fifty* hit a strong sex nerve located in the grey matter between our ears and in the vicinity of our underwear.

When I was an editor at *Playgirl* in the nineties it seemed to me that women were not *as interested* in erotic content or photos of attractive half-dressed or naked men—not the way men classically have been interested in erotic content and photos, anyway.

These days, women are sharing photos of handsome models and actors with their shirts off (and more), and posting about their affection and longing for Christian Grey—and other fictional characters — using racy sentiments and lots of bold comments. What I've observed while running the *Fifty Shades of Grey News* fan page and others is even a mere glimpse at the "happy trail" of a sexy, well-built male will elicit hundreds of comments the equivalent of cat calls, but this is all part of the new permission for women to be lusty and sexually expressive.

Fifty Shades of Grey seems to have lifted the lid off of female sexuality.

Readers got so attached to the handsome, kinky, antihero that casting of the movie that followed the books was a painful controversy. For over a year there was endless speculation about which actor would play Mr. Grey in the upcoming *Fifty Shades of Grey* movie (Matt Bomer, Ian Somerhalder and Henry Cavill were among fan favorites). There was an outcry of protest when actor Charlie Hunam got the role. And there was tension but, ultimately, more acceptance when Hunam quit and actor Jamie Dornan was hired. The fan reaction about who would win the role created an emotional uproar. They are still talking about it!

One of the qualities that first separated the *Fifty Shades of Grey* trilogy from other reading material is, upon completion, it caused a serious book hangover. This motivated women to read the trilogy over and over again, or look for books that could at least "take the edge off" of *Fifty Shades* withdrawal. (Since then I have read and heard of other books that have the similar book hangover impact, but many people remember *Fifty* as being their first.)

Comments like this one, from Rachael Brown, on the *Fifty Shades of Grey News* fan page on Facebook, were not unusual in social media during the height of Christian Grey mania: *"Yes I am slightly obsessed with Mr. Grey. I have now read the books 5 times and really considered starting for the sixth. I just can't seem to stop thinking about him... Maybe a spanking and a visit to the red room would help."*

Some readers say they've read the trilogy 10, 15, 25, and even 37 times! One of the most striking qualities of this amazing devotion to a fictional character is that fans talk about him *as if he is real*. Perhaps the same way we may think of Carrie Bradshaw (Sarah Jessica Parker) from *Sex in the City* or how we think of Harry Potter, Edward Cullen, or any favorite literary, TV, or movie character.

Although many of the fans of *Twilight* who came over to the *Fifty Shades* camp had already experienced a deep connection to a fictional character and world, those fans —and all the new ones — were getting a huge dose of arousal along with the love story.

The arousal factor—and how the books made women "randy"— was something this culture had not seen on such a large scale before. In a world in which we were still more accustomed to erotic material for men, the *Fifty Shades* books offered a splendid, detailed, delicious peek into unabashed female pleasure.

Part Two:

Attraction, Desire, and Falling in Love
As Experienced by Anastasia Steele and
Christian Grey
In *Fifty Shades of Grey*

*(Excerpts from my final paper for
Theories of Love and Romance class)*

Chapter 2

The Love Story that is *Fifty Shades*

Many women say when they read *Fifty Shades of Grey* it's easy to get caught up in the sexy storyline about the love affair between protagonists Christian Grey and Anastasia Steele.

He's described as a gorgeous, fit, sexy, generous, multitalented, multibillionaire who could easily be defined as a perfect man—except for a deep dark secret (he's into BDSM) and a difficult childhood that left him damaged.

She is an attractive, shy, unworldly virgin who works part time in a hardware store, and does not think she is beautiful or special, but of course, she is both.

Anastasia, 21, meets Christian, 27, while interviewing him for her school paper just before she is about to graduate from college. She is still an innocent. He seems distant and arrogant. She is clumsy and shy (she literally falls into his office and has to be assisted by Mr. Grey to stand up), yet, from the moment their hands touch, electricity happens and you know, by page 8, that something special is afoot.

Thus begins the attraction that leads to the love story that takes us through the books in the trilogy and compels us to follow the roller coaster of love that is the stormy yet deeply passionate and profoundly loving relationship between Christian and Ana.

When the story begins, Christian is a sexual dominant who does not engage in love relationships and Anastasia is a virgin who has never had a relationship.

They were drawn to each other from the first moment, however, what Christian first proposes to Ana was a rather shocking, "exchange relationship" (Kassin, Fein, Markus, 2008, p. 324) in which he would take care of her financially, supply her with all the comforts of life, and look after her in all ways. However, not as a boyfriend: he would be her dominant and, she, his submissive.

There was a NDA (Non-disclosure agreement) as well as an extensive business contract to sign. It was to be a purely sexual arrangement and in exchange Ana was to allow him to do whatever he pleased—within the clear contractual boundaries he described as "hard limits" and "soft limits."

Ana was open-minded but she wanted "more"—essentially a "communal relationship" (Kassin, Fein, Markus, 2008, p. 324) where they would be there for each other as romantic partners. They spent a good deal of time negotiating their agreement only to discard it as they found their way toward true affection, romance, love, and what many readers agree was *extremely satisfying sex.*

While women worldwide seem to enjoy the sex in the trilogy, many say the most moving part is the love story – and how Christian and Ana's attraction and trust in one another built over time.

"I believe what made their love so beautiful is the trust they had for one another," said Elisha Shell, commenting on the *Fifty Shades of Grey News.* "It was rocky at first but they experience so many beautiful firsts together."

Jessica Far pointed out, "The intense, sexy, emotional connection they shared was amazing but what I liked most is that they changed for each other and compromised. And that to me is what makes a relationship work!"

Ultimately, in true romance book fashion, we come to a perfect ending where everyone lives happily ever after. This story evokes strong emotions and reactions in readers and has been credited with enhancing the love lives of those who read it.

"Reading the books has made a change in me," commented Angela Wrightly on *Fifty Shades of Grey News*. "I want to do more for my husband outside of the bedroom too to make him happy. One of the things I love about these books is how Christian worships Ana."

Chapter 3

Controversy vs. Top Female Fantasy

As we all know, Christian's penchant for kinky sex and his behavior in some parts of the book is very controversial in some camps.

While Christian and Ana must get over many hurdles as they pursue their love – i.e., the physical and emotional conflicts established and set forth by the author — many of their emotions and experiences could mirror real life and real feelings.

While most women will not *really* be negotiating with a billionaire about whether they will accept the terms of his desired BDSM (Bondage, Domination, and Sadomasochism) relationship, the negotiations at the start of the trilogy create engaging communication and banter between the characters. It is not impossible to think that partners could have opposing goals in a relationship and that they must try to understand each other while attempting to chip away at the obstacles. In addition, the brain chemistry, hormones, pheromones — and feelings in the descriptions and dialog between Ana and Christian throughout the trilogy — could be part of the passion and conflicts of a real life couple. A reader wants to keep turning the page because she can relate to this couple and can become part of their intimacy.

The book also touches on some of the most popular female fantasies:

- The fantasy of being taken by a man and under his control
- The fantasy of letting someone powerful have their way with you
- The fantasy of the knight in shining armor showing up to rescue and romance you.

Add to that the fantasy that most readers would like to have happen in real life: Having a man who pays deep attention to you and your needs, as well as skillfully pleasuring you in ways that do not require an explanation or a request. *He just knows.*

The book also stimulates a fantasy and perhaps a hope, for many readers, of having their own Christian Grey. Aside from some of his difficult childhood issues and sexual paraphilia (meaning his sexual arousal and gratification depends on extreme sexual behavior readers have come to identify as kinky), he is pretty much the ultimate hot romance genre fantasy man – gorgeous beyond words, sexy, great lover, devoted Alpha male who won't take no for an answer. And a billionaire.

In the book, when Ana relays her inner dialog and shares the sensations of a look, a touch, a kiss, a sex act, or a conversation, readers are right there with her. We are perhaps, relating to her, or wishing to be her.

Readers are swept into a world of sexual unfolding for young Ana, and the opening of the heart of Mr. Grey. In the process there is a great deal of romance, passion, heated emotion, and enticing sexual activities, as well as love. There is conversation, good music, a storyline that never sleeps and a romance that takes us on a rollercoaster ride.

Fifty Shades of Grey has evoked a strong reaction in people.

Because Christian is wild and unpredictable, Ana never knows what to expect next, nor does the reader. In an interview in the *Herald Sun* in Australia, noted feminist writer Naomi Wolf, author of *Vagina: A New Biography*, suggested that there is a great sexual appeal in "otherness, wildness and the dimensions of the unknown."

Chapter 4

How Our Brain's Perceive Fiction

Anyone who has ever experienced "getting lost" in a great romance story knows it is as if you are actually *in the experience* with the hero and heroine.

You literally feel that first stir of attraction, that first kiss, and that magnetic pull that joins two characters together as they fall more deeply in love. You can even feel like you are right there in the scenes of passionate love-making and you can feel their tension, misunderstandings, and conflicts as well—strongly!

Independent of *Fifty Shades of Grey*, recent studies have explored the impact of fictional characters in the lives of fans, as well as how the brain perceives these characters and their experiences. The outcome: When you read a book, as far as the brain is concerned, it is really happening. You are there in the story.

This may explain why readers can get so carried away by *Fifty Shades* — or any good romance book — and experience so many emotions.

In one study, published in *The Journal of Personality and Social Psychology*, researchers at Ohio State University examined what happened to people who, while reading a fictional story, found themselves feeling the emotions, thoughts, beliefs and internal responses of one of the characters as if they were their own - a phenomenon the researchers call "experience-taking."

The *Research News*, at Ohio State, reported, "Experience-taking changes us by allowing us to merge our own lives with those of the characters we read about, which can lead to good outcomes," said Geoff Kaufman, who led the study as a graduate student at Ohio State. He said while this phenomenon does not occur with every reader, and it can be temporary, it is enabled to occur when, "people are able, in a sense, to forget about themselves and their own self-concept and self-identity while reading."

This seems to fit with the experience of *Fifty Shades of Grey* readers who report that the books are a total distraction; and that while engrossed in reading they don't even want to have to deal with life – work, kids, etc. It may also support one of the marital perks reported by *Fifty Shades* enthusiasts — the book has acted as an aphrodisiac and has offered an opportunity for "experiencing taking" that can bring a spark back to marital beds, according some psychologists and sex therapists.

In March 2012, *The New York Times* reported on two studies that found a marriage between neuroscience and fiction. The article, "Your Brain on Fiction," summarized a 2006 study published in the journal *NeuroImage*, that involved researchers in Spain, and also reported on a team of researchers from Emory University in the United States who shared their findings in the February 2012 *Brain & Language*. The article concluded that:

"The brain, it seems, does not make much of a distinction between reading about an experience and encountering it in real life; in each case, the same neurological regions are stimulated."It quoted Keith Oatley, an emeritus professor of cognitive psychology at the University of Toronto (and a published novelist), who suggested that a vivid simulation of reality "runs on minds of readers just as computer simulations run on computers."

The New York Times surmised: "Fiction — with its redolent

details, imaginative metaphors and attentive descriptions of people and their actions — offers an especially rich replica. Indeed, in one respect novels go beyond simulating reality to give readers an experience unavailable off the page: the opportunity to enter fully into other people's thoughts and feelings. The novel, of course, is an unequaled medium for the exploration of human social and emotional life. And there is evidence that just as the brain responds to depictions of smells and textures and movements as if they were the real thing, so it treats the interactions among fictional characters as something like real-life social encounters. "

These three studies offer remarkable insight into the level of involvement with the books and characters that many fans seem to report — including why so many women talk about Christian Grey as if he is real.

"What do you mean he's fictional?" said Jenny Cocchi, on *Fifty Shades of Grey News*, in response to a question about whether or not women are too obsessed with this fictional character.

I spoke with Daniel Amen, MD, about the effects of reading *Fifty Shades of Grey*.

Dr. Amen is a clinical neuroscientist and psychiatrist. As founder of the Amen Clinics and bestselling author of 30 books, including *Unleash the Power of the Female Brain: Supercharging Yours for Better Health, Energy, Mood, Focus, and Sex,* he is an expert on understanding, optimizing, and harnessing the power of the female brain. Dr. Amen is also the author of the bestselling book, *The Brain and Love*.

He confirms that the brain *does* believe fiction is real!

"Yes," he said. "You have to be careful what you read. I think you have to be careful what you read because it becomes part of your DNA. It stimulates people."

So how does Christian Grey, specifically, get into a woman's brain?

"[Through] Happy thoughts," he said. "He becomes part of the synapses. You're much more likely to remember something if it's visual and emotionally intense, good or bad. For that month my wife was reading those three books, I noticed that she was more talkative, happier, and more edgier, and was very curious."

He explained that women love reading *Fifty Shades* so much that it can heighten the feel good brain chemical dopamine and inspire more sexual activity at home, which in turn helps women feel better. It's not just the book, it's the touching, eye contact, and intimacy it may lead to.

As Dr. Amen put it: "Dopamine is the chemical that is pleasure, surprise, motivation, 'OMG, I can't believe he did that,' or 'I can't believe she's giving into him.' I think husbands or boyfriends get the benefit because now it helps the women relax."

Can reading in general have that impact on fans and make people feel the love, sex, and flirtation is really happening in their lives?

"It depends on the book," he said. "Ken Follett is great about writing about relationships and you find yourself totally immersed and it's like you are there. This is why you smile and why you laugh – because he's talented at being able to put you right where the story is … right where the bedroom is … right where the flirtatious woman or guy is."

Chapter 5

The Siren Song of *Fifty Shades*:

Erotic Triggers and Appealing to all the Senses

So what was it that touched such a deep longing in readers? What is the secret sauce that made so many go gaga for Mr. Grey?

In search of insight into what got readers so hooked, I attended an informative lecture by sex therapist Sari Cooper, LCSW. Titled "Fifty Shades of Grey: What You Can Learn about Sex Esteem from the Bestseller," it was delivered to an audience of psychoanalysts at Washington Square Institute in New York City (tough crowd, by the way).

Cooper, a columnist for *Psychology Today* and an ASECT certified sex therapist, said she was even using the book to help couples. It was a rare opportunity to gain insight from a professional who had studied the trilogy closely and was in fact utilizing it as a tool in sex therapy.

She offered a compelling view on why she felt the books were so successful by outlining what she called "the erotic triggers" that are written into the book. She contended that these triggers combined are what kept the heroine of the story so stimulated and intrigued, and made the story so irresistible to the readers.

"These are the multisensory messages that our bodies receive and that get us turned-on."

She was kind enough to give me permission to use her direct

quotes in my college paper and related articles and writings. Here are the 10 erotic triggers she outlined.

1. **Powerful hero**. "He is dark, mysterious, and possibly dangerous — a total Alpha male. He's wild, dangerous, and unpredictable. Being with him is like a rollercoaster ride."

2. **Awakened Heroine**. "She is innocent. She is the yin to the yang of Christian Grey. She is a young woman awakened by this man who knows a lot more."

3. **Christian uses all the senses – taste, touch, sight, scent, sound**. "For example, Ana is always talking about how he smells and he about her scent. He also consciously uses these different triggers to arouse her."

4. **Music is a huge part of it**. There are many musical moments in the book that inspire erotic or emotionally charged moments.

5. **He appeals to her psychologically**. "He sends signals to throw her off balance, such as his first gift of the collector's edition of *Tess of the d'Urbervilles*. He attaches a quote from the book that says there may be danger waiting. It creates more intrigue for her and she is intrigued by him."

6. **There is stimulation of all the erogenous zones and multisensory anticipation**. "Christian does it with such expertise, and so much foreplay, with plenty of time to get Anastasia ready."

   A. **Primary erogenous zones**: Genitals and breasts.
   B. **Secondary erogenous zones**: Earlobe, neck.
   C. **Tertiary erogenous zones**: Feet, arms, scalp.

7. **BDSM.** "The book has opened up the door a crack to things people may not have considered before. In *Fifty Shades* Ana has many fears about being hurt, but when she is in the red room of pain she is not just in pain — she is in a state of arousal beyond what she would normally feel. Sexual arousal sometimes involves working with negative emotions such as fear and anxiety. It's the experience of being on a roller coaster that enhances the state of arousal."

8. **Love.** "Ana pushes for 'more' than being his submissive and he 'tries' because he will do anything to keep her. He's only had subs before, women that he has controlled, and he is pushed to his hard limits by Ana who is demanding more. That's what people love about the book. They want the romance, the emotional tension. Will it work out for them? They want to know!"

9. **The experience of being desired.** "This is a huge erotic trigger for women. It's the experience of being that special someone. There is no one else in his eyes. He only has eyes for her. She is the one he longs for. It combines the erotic with the sensual. Being desired is such a turn on for women."

10. **He's very loyal.** "At first we are not sure if we can trust him. She talks about his 'stalker tendencies.' What wins Ana over, and wins the reader over, is he's very loyal. And when she needs him, he's there. I think it works because women can feel the fantasy of having that danger, with the security of having a good relationship."

Cooper's analysis (above) made perfect sense to me in both understanding what the character of Ana experienced and how the readers, too, took that rollercoaster ride into the erotic and the psychologically intrigue. The idea that women can experience the fantasy with Ana, yet view it from the safety of their own relationships, also explains the appeal of the books.

I wanted to research more about "erotic triggers" to back up what Cooper said. In the book *A Billion Wicked Thoughts*, authors Ogi Igas and Sai Gaddam, point out how the sexual cues from men and women are very different.

"Women are more focused on emotional and psychological cues which generate erotic stories suited for satisfying female appetites," they write. "Women respond to a truly astonishing range of cues across many domains. The physical appearance of a man, his social status, personality, commitment, the authenticity of his emotions, his confidence, family, attitude toward children, kindness, height, and smell are all important. Unlike men, who become aroused after being exposed to a single cue, women need to experience enough simultaneous cues to cross an ever-varying threshold" (Igas & Gaddam, 2011, p. 212).

Looking back into the pages of the books, it is clear that Christian is excited the moment he *sees* Ana, continues to be so, and could have sex with her anywhere, any time. Sensitive as he is to her needs, his attraction to her if fairly typical (in a stereotypical way) of male desire. "I don't need an aphrodisiac when I am near you," he says. "I think you know that, and I think you react the same when you are around me" (James, 2012, 291).

Once initiated, it doesn't take Ana long to feel responsive, however, there are a host of different kinds of cues that begin her arousal — a look from Christian, something he says, the way he smells, his touch, the music. It keeps both Ana, and the reader, in a state of anticipation. Here are some examples of the use of the senses from *Fifty Shades of Grey*:

- **Sound**: "You are mine," he whispers, "only mine. Don't forget it." His voice is intoxicating, his words heady, seductive" (James, 2012, 119).

- **Sight**: "A slow, sexy smile spreads across his lovely face, and I am rendered speechless as my insides melt. He is without a doubt the most beautiful man on the planet, too beautiful for the little people below, too beautiful for me" (James, 2012, 370).

- **Touch and Scent**: "He runs the tips of his finger down my cheek. Oh my. His proximity, his delicious Christian smell. We're supposed to be talking but my heart is pounding, my blood singing as it courses through my body, desire pooling, unfurling … everywhere. Christian bends and runs his nose along my shoulder and up the base of my ear, his fingers slipping into my hair" (James, 2012, 427).

The reader is constantly barraged with these triggers or cues; along with a genuine emotional connection between the characters, these are present from the start. Even if the dialog is sometimes a little corny (Ana does have some of the corniest lines in the book), the sentiments can set women's hearts afire because they stimulate the fantasy of the perfect man who is not only gorgeous and rich, but who is sexually masterful and desires her pleasure (Sigh).

Chapter 6

Was it Falling in Love — or Just Crazy Attraction — at First Sight?

One of the exciting aspects of *Fifty Shades of Grey* is that everything happened so quickly. But was it actually love at first sight?

I believe it was.

Essentially, they had each other at hello — although neither of them were familiar enough with love to recognize it in that moment.

Although there was a bit of a back and forth dance that led to the start of their relationship, from the moment they met the connection was strong. As the characters reveal their emotions to themselves, and one another, we see that this really was love at first sight, according to recent discoveries about love and how it impacts the brain.

After her first meeting with Christian, Ana has a strong physical reaction to Mr. Grey — and he to her. Because it is so unfamiliar, it frightens her so she tries to get away, right after interviewing him. With heart pounding she heads for the elevator and tries to leave the building. "No man has ever affected me the way Christian Grey has, and I cannot fathom why," she muses to herself. "Is it his looks? His civility? Wealth? Power? I don't understand my irrational reaction. I breathe an enormous sigh of relief. What in heaven's name was that all about? I valiantly attempt to calm down and gather my thoughts. I shake my head. What was *that*?" (James, 2012, p. 17).

These two are irresistibly drawn to each other. For Ana, it manifests in physical symptoms that make her feel out of control and unable to speak intelligently; she finds herself succumbing to woozy clumsiness and falling, in reaction to Christian.

These all appear symptomatic of falling in love, according to a meta-analysis study conducted by Syracuse University Professor Stephanie Ortigue that revealed falling in love can elicit not only the same euphoric feeling as using cocaine, but also affects intellectual areas of the brain. The researchers also found falling in love only takes about a fifth of a second!

These findings seemed to mirror the awkwardness of Ana and Christian's first meeting – he was cool and collected on the outside but he later revealed how taken he was and she was obviously overwrought by feelings in those first moments. While she kept thinking he was arrogant and annoying, her body seemed to be having a different kind of reaction.

According to an October 22, 2010 report in *Science Daily*, "Results from Ortigue's team revealed when a person falls in love, 12 areas of the brain work in tandem to release euphoria-inducing chemicals such as dopamine, oxytocin, adrenaline and vasopressin. The love feelings also affects sophisticated cognitive functions, such as mental representation, metaphors and body image."

The researcher was asked if the heart or brain fall in love and Ortigue responded: "I would say the brain, but the heart is also related because the complex concept of love is formed by both bottom-up and top-down processes from the brain to the heart and vice versa. For instance, activation in some parts of the brain can generate stimulations to the heart, butterflies in the stomach. Some symptoms we sometimes feel as a manifestation of the heart may sometimes be coming from the brain."

Ana was in Christian's office for under an hour during that first meeting, yet she experienced so much stimulation from the cascade of brain chemicals that she was overcome by her reaction to him — much in the way that Professor Ortigue described.

Chapter 7

Explaining the Electricity
Between Heroine and Hero

Anastasia, who is the narrator of the book, speaks often about the almost-electrical response she has when she and Christian touch. She says this about the special "moment" of their first meeting in Christian's office: "I place my hand in his and we shake. As our fingers touch, I feel an odd, exhilarating shiver run through me. I withdraw my hand, embarrassed. Must be static. I blink rapidly, my eyelids matching my heart rate" (James, 2012, p. 8).

Ana does not realize, at first, that the electricity is a signal of arousal because she is not sexually experienced. This kind of experience is very seductive, says psychologist Robert J. Sternberg in his book, *Cupid's Arrow*. "Arousal can start very fast. Evidence suggests that people start feeling expectations about romantic possibilities toward each other within a fraction of meeting these others. In other words, passionate love at first sight is really at first sight, possibly starting to arise in a mere matter of moments" (Sternberg, 1998, p. 114).

Maryanne Fisher, Ph.D. says women have over ten times the number of touch receptors in their hands than men and the receptors in a woman's hands are closer together than in a man's (Fisher and Costello, 2010, p. 46).

She describes the chemical reaction to touch in this way: "Once a nerve ending of the skin is stimulated, a message goes directly to the thalamus, which acts as a relay station, then to the primary sensory cortex area (parietal lobe). Each area of the strip corresponds to a different location in the body: Fingers, genitals, and so on. When a message is received in the primary sensory cortex, another message is promptly relayed back out to the hypothalamus and the pituitary gland, thus triggering the release of oxytocin, the hormone of contentment and bonding."

Throughout *the Fifty Shades of Grey* trilogy, Ana and Christian's chemistry is strong and a simple touch from Christian continues to stimulate intense reactions. This brings Ana (and readers!) great bliss, it also adds to the intrigue and makes Christian Grey impossible to resist. Here are two examples:

In this scene, Ana is sitting next to Christian in the back seat of his car as they are being driven somewhere. "His thumb strokes my knuckles back and forth, and my heart skips a beat as my breathing accelerates. How does he do this to me? He's only touching a very small area of my body, and the hormones are flying" (James, 2012, p. 86). Moments later, they step into an elevator to get to the helicopter pad so Christian (also a skilled pilot) can fly Ana to his apartment in Seattle: "I try to keep my face impassive as we enter the elevator," she says. "The doors close, and it's there, the weird electrical attraction crackling between us, enslaving me" (James, 2012, p. 87).

Judith Horstman, writing in *The Scientific American Book on Love, Sex, and the Brain*, explains that our human brains truly do set up a chemical reaction that trips off a sensory experience. "When people who are smitten with love or lust they say there is a chemistry or electricity between them, they speak the truth," she writes. "The brain (and your love life) is powerfully effected by honest-to-goodness sparks — tiny amounts of electricity created by chemical reactions that transmit information among your neurons" (Horstman, 2012, p. 23).

Neurotransmitters and hormones fan the flames and this is what helps these small, electrical touches and moments turn into full-blown passion.

Because Ana is completely inexperienced when she first meets Christian, she has no clear understanding of "sparks flying." However, it soon becomes a state of being for her. The reader goes along for the ride and, through Ana's eyes, experiences attraction, desire, and the youthful exuberance of sexual and romantic awakening.

Chapter 8

Love Chemicals and the Kiss that Began it All

In fairytales, the kiss is the thing that can awaken the sleeping princess or turns the frog or beast back into a prince. Ana wanted that! But in *Fifty Shades of Grey* it was a refused kiss that first fueled the flames of Ana's intrigue and desire.

Christian invited Ana for coffee, and on the way back to his hotel she is nearly run over by a speeding cyclist. Christian catches her from falling and pulls her into his arms. They stare into one another's eyes, captivated. "And for the first time in my twenty-one years, I want to be kissed. I want to feel his mouth on mine" (James, 2012, p. 48).

They are both deeply drawn and moved by this moment, but Christian, knowing her innocence and his own darkness, refuses to kiss her. "Anastasia, you should steer clear of me. I'm not the man for you," he whispers (James, 2012, p. 48). She leaves the situation fearing she's misread his interest and he leaves even more desirous of her.

When they finally do kiss, it is in an uncontained eruption of passion and it is the action that fully launches the erotic adventure between Christian and Ana — and the reader. It occurs at the Heathman Hotel, before the characters have had a sexual experience, and before Ana has signed the NDA (Non-disclosure agreement) Christian insisted must be in place before their relationship could begin.

Since paperwork and agreements were a huge part of book one in the trilogy, this scene showed the sheer force of their attraction and illustrates so many of the erotic cues Sari Cooper discussed earlier. The passage in the book has become legendary among fans. It is there that we see them walk in silence to the elevator, step in quietly, and then find themselves in a cauldron of uncontained desire. She looks up at him demurely, he feasts his eyes on her hungrily, and then, after all his insistence about getting her desires in writing, he just tosses it all to the wind so he can seize the moment and utters one of the most famous lines in the book.

"'Oh, fuck the paperwork,' he growls" (James, 2012, p. 77-78). He lunges, grabs her hands in a vise like grip, presses them against the wall, and kisses her ... hard.

When the elevator stops and the kiss abruptly ends, they walk out to the lobby: "I struggle to keep up with him because my wits have been thoroughly and royally scattered all over the floors and walls of elevator three in the Heathman Hotel." Ana goes off to work still reeling from the experience. "The memory of our kiss this morning comes back to haunt me. I have thought of nothing else all day ... To say I was distracted would be the understatement of the year" (James, 2012, p. 87).

Understanding the chemistry of a kiss can help explain the desire and sexual awakening Ana went through, as well as why she felt fragmented afterwards, and distracted, because the kiss ended suddenly.

In *The Science of Kissing*, Sheril Kirshenbaum says that a lot goes on in the body before a kiss, and a tremendous amount occurs once the lips touch. "During a passionate kiss, our blood vessels dilate and receive more oxygen than normal to the brain. Our breathing becomes irregular and deepens; our cheeks flush, our pulse quickens, and our pupils dilate, which may be one reason so many of us close our eyes" (Kirshenbaum, 2011, 78).

"Perhaps most important of all, when we kiss, all five of our senses are busy transmitting messages to the brain. Billions of little nerve connections are at work, firing away and distributing signals around our bodies. Eventually, these signals reach what is called the somatosensory cortex: the region of the brain that processes feelings of touch, temperature, pain, and more. Here they are interpreted, resulting in thought such as: 'Did he just have onions?' or 'where is that hand wandering?'" (Kirshenbaum, 2011, 79).

Ana was pretty taken with where his hands wandered and this kiss set the stage for the passion that would ensue. "A kiss is more than a kiss," writes Judith Horstman. "It is an intimate exchange of scents, tastes, textures, secrets, and emotions. A touch of the lips triggers a cascade of neural messages and chemicals that transmit tactile sensations and sensual excitement, feelings of closeness, motivation, and even euphoria."

Chapter 9

Love Grows and Emotional Connection Builds Online

As the relationship unfolds, Ana and Christian evolve their love affair through romantic banter and conversation via e-mail. Christian buys Ana a computer, a Blackberry and an iPad so they can stay in constant touch.

She is bolder in her e-mail communication than in person. His dominant spirit comes out more, but also his concern for her well-being. It's all very sexy, romantic, and moves the relationship forward—and also starts some fights. After a trying e-mail discussion one day she e-mails, "It was nice knowing you" and, within minutes, Christian shows up at her house (and she is happy he does)! During the work day, there is also a great deal of recounting sensual times together, and anticipating those to come. Some important messages about true feelings are also delivered by e-mail.

In *Love Online*, Aaron Ben-ze've says that even in exclusively cyber love or cybersex relationships "one important aspect of the relationship is similar … the emotion of love is experienced as fully and as intensely as in an offline relationship." So it makes sense that as Christian and Ana's relationship grew, the use of e-mail helped to keep their hearts connected, and also kept them aroused.

Use of e-mail as a device to keep the dialog going between Christian and Ana all day long was a new twist on a classic courtship tool. "Falling in love through letter writing is not a new phenomenon: It has been going on for hundreds of years. ... Online relationships are based on an improved version of the old-fashioned way of communicating: writing. In the new version, the time gap between writing, sending, receiving, and reading has been made almost instantaneous — the sender can receive a reply while still in a state of emotions in which she sent the original message. This difference, which may appear merely technical, is of great emotional significance, as emotions are brief and involve the urge to act immediately" (Ben-ze've, 2004, p. 7).

It really makes sense that in modern relationships, e-mail communication can light a fire in a romance, and can also create a call to action. It was that emotion of the moment that inspired Ana's e-mail of mock break-up to Christian and that compelled Christian to hop in his car, take it up with Ana in person, and reintroduce her to his seductive ways to erase the possibility of her breaking-up with him.

Readers can surely relate to the fun of having someone to "sext" with from the office, or sending or receiving the occasional love letter by e-mail. This form of communication added to the excitement of Ana and Christian's day and kept them close, while keeping the reader entertained.

Chapter 10

Music and Dopamine Set the Stage for Pleasure

Music plays an important part in this love story, so much so that there was a huge playlist of *Fifty Shades of Grey* songs on YouTube.com and Spotify.com (with diverse songs such as "Sex on Fire," "Come Fly with Me," "You Put a Spell on Me") and author E.L. James released a CD classical songs ("Jesu," "Joy of Man's Desiring," "Cannon in D") mentioned in the book — all before there was even a movie out yet! Now, of course, the movie has been released with a sexy and hugely successful soundtrack, albeit different from some of the original songs mentioned in the book.

Christian loves music – whether he is tantalizing Ana with the sounds of Thomas Talis' "Fantasia" or "Spem in Alium" while he has her blindfolded and bound, or when he is at the piano playing "Adagio" at four in the morning when he cannot sleep. They also talk a lot about music they love, finding they both have classical and eclectic tastes, yet she is being exposed to new music through him all the time. He gives Ana a new iPad with a romantic playlist of favorites as a gift. In addition, Christian's use of music in erotic play helps stimulate all of Ana's senses – the readers too.

There is a certain joy that comes from music that moves the soul, opens the heart, or stirs sexual response and it can release the feel-good hormone dopamine into the system.

Jeffery P. Kahn explores music and dopamine in *Angst: Origins of*

Anxiety and Depression. "When people listen to music the resulting dopamine release makes people want to move in more than one way — they dance, but they also seek out pleasure, novelty, and inspiration ... music also helps babies to fall asleep and helps people feel better about their woes. Music is also a stimulus for love and seduction. 'If music be the food of love, play on' as William Shakespeare says in *Twelfth Night*. And he didn't even know about dopamine" (Kahn, 2012, p. 144).

"Dopamine is part of the reward system in the brain, and helps us form and recall emotional memories of things we like. When we find something we want (e.g. food, sex, etc.), some pleasurable dopamine is released in our brain. From then on, when we catch a hint of good things around us, dopamine tells us to go out looking for them" (Kahn, 2012, p. 143).

Music from *Fifty Shades*—both the book and movie—is something readers can bring into their homes, their mobile devices, and even onto their computers at work, keeping the fantasy of Christian and Ana alive long after they have finished the books. That rush of dopamine can be renewed by every familiar song or note, keeping readers connected to *Fifty Shades of Grey*. It may even inspire the search for a new "book boyfriend" in hopes of recreating that same rush felt with *Fifty Shades*.

Chapter 11

Why Ana is Intoxicated by Christian Grey's Scent

Ana is constantly speaking of the way Christian smells and how intoxicated — and comforted — she is by his scent. She finds him "intoxicating" and "inhales deeply" of the fresh smelling scent on his skin and the essence around him (James, 2012, p. 48).

In writing about infatuation in *The Anatomy of Love*, Helen Fisher, Ph. D., says that smell can spark strong physical and psychological reactions. "Between your eyes, within your skull, at the base of your brain, some five million olfactory neurons dangle from the roof of each nasal cavity, swaying in the air currents you inhale. These nerve cells transmit messages to the part of the brain that controls your sense of smell. But they also link up with the limbic system, a group of primitive structures in the middle of your brain that govern, fear, rage, hate, ecstasy, and lust. Because of the brain's wiring, smells have the potential to create intense erotic feelings" (Fisher, 1992, p. 43).

Christian's smell is very important to Ana, and, the scent of a man is key to women in mate selection. It makes sense this young, fertile woman would be drawn to, and aroused by, the scent of a man in possession of power and virility.

Biologist Randy Thornhill and psychologist Steven Gangestad suggest that smell is one of the simplest cues to genetic fitness. "Lots of studies have shown that the way a partner smells is an important factor in sexual attraction and mate selection, and women report they are more strongly affected by smells than men are (e.g. Herz & Chaill, 1997). To Thornhill and Gangestad, the idea that smell may be a good marker of genetic fitness helps explain the gender difference. Women should be more responsive to smell because they have the most interest in the genetic fitness of their partners" (Bradbury and Karney, 2010, p. 103). Women, they say, are most responsive to this marker during ovulation.

Ana and Christian seem to be chemically drawn to each other! Pheromones and androstenol are another explanation for such strong attraction.

An article on body scent attractiveness in men and women published in *Behavioral Ecology* reported that scent and pheromones have a big impact on attraction: "Several lines of evidence indicate that olfactory cues or pheromones may play a major role in the human sexual selection system. First, though adults of both sexes report that body scent of others significantly affects their sexual interest; women report a stronger effect than men" (Franzoi and Herzog, 1987; Herz and Cahill, 1997; Regan and Berscheid, 1995).

The journal article also points out that women have particular olfactory sensitivity to "androstenol and related chemicals," especially before ovulation. "Androstenol, a chemical precursor of androstenone, is an important contributor to body odor, and its production is highly sexually dimorphic; men excrete three times more androstenol in urine than do women" (Brooksbank, 1962; Brooksbank and Haslewood, 1961).

This could explain, in part, why Ana is always so captivated by his scent – or his presence – and why she is always trying to inhale him when they are in close quarters, lying next to each other, sitting next to each other, or when he leans over her.

Interestingly, *Behavioral Ecology* also mentions studies that revealed women's preference for the scent of symmetrical men when fertile, and female preference for the scents of facially attractive individuals. This also correlates with Ana's — and perhaps *everyone's* — attraction to the handsome Mr. Grey.

Chapter 12

Hormones and Why This Pair Can't Get Enough of One Another

They can't get enough of each other sexually, but it runs so much deeper.

Christian and Ana are unable to stay away from each other. He is a "love virgin" who has a lot of baggage — emotional, and the kind that comes with being a billionaire, as well as some odd relationships with ex-lovers — and she has a lot of fear about his dark side, yet they are so deeply connected and attached that they cannot stay apart.

Ana goes back and forth about whether she can love him ("I am Icarus too close to the sun and will get burned," is an oft repeated phrase), and Christian becomes more vulnerable as he falls deeply in love with her and thus wants to protect and possess her.

The rollercoaster of emotions that occur makes for a very interesting ride for readers. There are so many emotional ups and downs, and so many sex scenes in which something different and new is happening, that the readers has to keep turning the pages to see what happens next; they especially need to make sure these two, somehow, keep finding their way back to each other.

I think we can all, on some level, relate to that feeling of being so drawn to another person, especially in the throes of a new romance; and we can also relate to the yearning inspired by fictional characters in love. Don't we all want the characters to *finally* achieve the ultimate love connection and commitment and don't we long for them to find their happy ending? I know I wanted the book to end like a satisfying romantic movie!

Horstman compares love to heroin addiction and this comparison seems most fitting, especially where Christian Grey is concerned because he definitely has *heroine* addiction. He is smitten. Christian sighs, on many occasions, "Oh Miss Steele, what you do to me." In book one he says, "You intoxicate, Miss Steele, and you calm me. Such a heady combination" (James, 2012, p.482). Looking at Helen Fisher's description of different kinds of love in *Why We Love*, I would say that Christian's love, at first, seems to fall under *mania*, which she describes as "obsessive, jealous, irrational, possessive, dependent love. "However, Fisher adds, "Most people are exceedingly obsessive, illogical, and possessive when they are passionately in love" (Fischer, 2004, p. 95).

In *The Scientific American Book on Love, Sex, and the Brain*, Horstman offers what could explain the intoxicating chemical reaction Christian and Ana may be experiencing: "Love in your brain, then, is indeed a potent brew. It involves the blending and balance of more than 100 of those hormones and neurochemical messengers. Lust is driven by testosterone (in men and in women), norepinephrine gives an excitatory rush, and dopamine provides an over-the-moon high that rivals heroin in its orgasmic and addictive kick. These chemicals can so heighten the passion of sex and sexual craving that it becomes a basic need, such as hunger or thirst — so powerful it can feel like obsessive compulsive disorder" (Horstman, 2012, p. 23).

Christian's attachment appears to be over-possessive and co-dependent. But Ana, and the readers, cut him some slack because he also has a history that indicates a rough childhood and lost adolescence.

Because he has been so burned as a child, and because of his need to control, he can't stand being away from Ana for any length of time. Because his mother died in front of him when he was four-years-old and he could not save her, he has a great need to make sure he keeps Ana safe. For a good part of the trilogy, he exhibits "stalker–like tendencies" that Ana often jokes about — he will not let her out of his sight, or out of the sight of his security team. We come to know there is real danger he is protecting her from, but his worry and inability to stay away from her is epic.

In just the first week of their relationship Ana went to visit her mother in Georgia, to get away and think; she e-mailed that she missed him and he flew, via private plane, from Washington State to Georgia to see her. At other times, he or his team are always nearby. It drives her a little crazy, but she is also seduced by his desire to care for and be there for her. At one point, they have an epic break-up for a few days and this totally transforms Christian and sets him on the path of a committed romantic relationship free of contracts and dominance — because, as he puts it, he never wants to feel that way again.

In *The Psychology of Love*, Stanton Peele addresses love sickness in the chapter, "Fools for Love: The Romantic Ideal, Psychological Theory, and Addictive Love." I found this statement that applies to *Fifty Shades of Grey* and also the readers reaction to it. "The love described by social psychologists can take on the romantic glow of love as seen in cheap novels. In Berscheid and Walster's (1974) approach, love is a matter of sharing a special emotional — at times drug-like — state. The primary issues are finding the right love match and experiencing an otherworldly, untrammeled passion" (Peele, 1988, p. 166).

Fans, of course, would want to replace the use of the outdated phrase "cheap novels" with the more politically correct "best-selling erotic romance novels."

Throughout the *Fifty Shades of Grey* trilogy, Christian and Ana have an intense yearning for one another. They do have "untrammeled passion." It is appealing to readers because it speaks to the need to desire, and be desired by another — to be wanted.

Chapter 13

Under the Influence of The Big O ... Oxytocin

Ana and Christian are constantly having sex in *Fifty Shades*. I suspect most women would not be able to tolerate the sheer magnitude of it – not without some injury or occasional bladder infection – but Ana is young, nimble, and eager and Christian is a skilled lover.

Every sexual encounter between them culminates in one or more orgasms, for both partners, which means the release of oxytocin for these two is off the charts! This could explain why they fell in love with each other so hard and so quickly — they spent so much of their relationship basking in the embrace of each other and, what is affectionately known as "The cuddle hormone." It is understandable that readers went along for that ride with them.

Although oxytocin was often thought of as the bonding hormone between mother and child, it exists in both males and females and intensifies in the orgasmic experience.

Kerstin Uvnas Moberg, M.D., Ph.D. has studied this hormone extensively. In *The Oxytocin Factor* she writes, "Studies of human sexual relations have shown that oxytocin levels rise powerfully in the blood of both males and females, and reach maximum concentration with the release of orgasm. Oxytocin may also stimulate the muscle activity related to orgasm in both men and woman" (Moberg, 2003, p. 118).

Moberg says oxytocin is responsible for making people feel calm, relaxed and even sleepy after intercourse. It has been known to make women want to cuddle after lovemaking, and give both partners the feeling that they cherish remaining close and connected in sexual afterglow. "With oxytocin pulsating through your bloodstream, it seems that this love will last forever. Often at this point, partners speak of how much they mean to each other" (Moberg, 2003, p. 119).

The risk with oxytocin released with orgasms, she writes, is that it can enhance emotional bonds even for those who are not sure if they are right for each other. But in the long run, "a solid sexual relationship promotes feelings of increased security and decreased anxiety in the mating partners" (Moberg, 2003, p. 120). Luckily, Ana and Christian found their way to an enduring love.

Chapter 14

Fulfilling the Triangular Theory of Love-Intimacy, Passion and Commitment

One of the most satisfying aspects of the trilogy is the fact that this couple does make it, and in a grand way. The overall story satisfies our desire to see this couple engage in a great love affair with great sex, family life, intimacy and commitment. The fulfillment of their union brings them both maturity and healing, as well a true balance. They go on to formulate a healthy family life, a sustainable love and commitment, and a blending of their two sexual worlds – "hearts and flowers" along with a little BDSM fun.

Sternberg's "Triangular Theory of Love" applies well to the relationship that develops between Ana and Christian — you can literally see them evolving toward it, and then living it, as you read through each book of the trilogy. The sense of completion and balance is appealing to the reader, and may inspire the longing for such a relationship in their own lives. As Sternberg points out in *Cupid's Arrow*: "A substantial body of evidence suggests that the components of intimacy, passion, and commitment play a key role in love over and above other attributes."

Here are some of the ways this theory can be interpreted in the relationship between these characters.

Intimacy. Before they even started dating, Christian and Ana seemed to have a very intimate connection. The first time they shared an evening in bed had nothing to do with sex. Ana, not a big drinker, was out celebrating her graduation and made a drunken call to Christian, who immediately sped to her locale, basically saved her from an unwanted advance by another man, held her head as she threw up, and took her back to his hotel to keep her safe. He slept in the same bed, but did not touch her. In the period between books one and two, Christian and Ana mature a great deal as they share many firsts together and learn to love together. They still grapple with control and self-esteem issues, but they talk things through constantly (something readers love — he cares so much about her feelings). Over time, they truly develop an emotional transparency with one another, sharing their truth and allowing them to be completely vulnerable with one another. By the end of the trilogy they exhibit all of Sternberg's 10 descriptions of intimacy, "those feelings in a relationship that promote closeness, bondedness, and connectedness" (Sternberg, 1998, p.6-8).

1. **Desiring to promote the welfare of the loved one.** Christian is obsessed with Ana's well-being, comfort, and health. Among other big ways he shows this, he is constantly asking, "Did you eat?," "Are you hungry?" and telling her she has to eat. Ana is constantly searching for information on his "issues" so she can help him. She has deep compassion for Christian and his emotional issues and sees herself as an agent there to bring him from the darkness into the light.

2. **Experiencing Happiness with the Loved One.** When they are not dealing with some of the crazy shenanigans perpetuated by antagonists, they have a good life together. One highlight was when he took her hang gliding (he

piloted) and said. "I want to chase the dawn with you" (James, 2012, p. 443).

3. **Holding the loved one in high regard**. Christian is in awe of Ana's courage and her acceptance of him, his "special" needs, and his rather large emotional baggage. At one point he sends an e-mail that begins: "Dear Miss Steele, You are quite simply exquisite. The most beautiful, intelligent, witty, and brave woman I have ever met ..." (James, 2012, p. 281). Ana also encourages him to step into his own greatness, and get beyond low self-esteem rather than perpetuating the personal mythology that he is "damaged goods."

4. **Being able to count on the loved one in times of need**. While there is a white-knight-damsel-in-distress element to Christian's Alpha approach to always *being there* (or keeping tabs on his beloved), they are there for each other. After Ana fights off a pass from her boss, she comes out of her office building, weak and falls in front of the building. Christian and his security chief are there in a nanosecond and they head up to rough up the man who tried to hurt her. He has a tendency to be "mercurial" when things slip out of his control and she has a tendency to question the relationship a lot at the start, but, overall, he turns out to be solid, as does Ana, in a crisis — even when it is painful. The whole book is about them overcoming one problem after another — often with danger lurking — so there are many times when she wants to leave, and could leave, but decides her love is strong enough to see them through. Christian is overly committed from the start and wants to care for her and protect her. The one time he lets her down in a major way is toward the end of the last book when she discovers she is

pregnant. He freaks out in overblown anger, but then comes around. We learn that much of his fear is about being a parent, since his experience with his birth mother was so devastating.

5. **Having mutual understanding with the loved one.** He learns to read her like a favorite book, and she spends much time trying to figure out and understand him. Once Christian realizes he loves her and wants the "more" that she has requested, they bend to meet each other half way. Mutual understanding grows with their relationship.

6. **Sharing oneself and ones possessions with the loved one.** Christian is a self-made billionaire and extremely generous. Ana is not into his money and in the beginning fights with him about the gifts he insists on giving her. She wants more of him than his gifts — and she gets both, over time. When they marry, he refuses to have a pre-nup and says what is his is now hers. One very telling part of their love story is when Ana was attempting to help save Christian's sister from harm and needed an immediate five million dollars for a kidnapper. She went to the bank to make a withdrawal, and Christian thought she wanted the cash because she was leaving him. He got on the phone with her and said, sincerely, "Is it enough?" and told the bank to give her whatever she wanted.

7. **Receiving emotional support from the loved one.** One of the key expressions in the book, from Christian to Ana, is when he admits, "I am Fifty Shades of F—ked up." Ana is constantly trying to get information about why Christian is the way he is — and even sees his therapist to gain insights

— and when she hears the story from him she becomes his healer. He empowers her to have greater self-esteem and she lifts him from his dark past. One big part of the story is he refuses to be touched on his chest; we learn this is because his mother's pimp put cigarettes out on his skin as a child. Ana slowly and lovingly creates trust that makes him *want her* to touch him and help him past his fear of the memories

8. **Giving emotional support to the loved one.** They both do this in their own ways, especially in trying to empower each other beyond insecurities. Ana begins the journey unsure why he would want her, because she saw herself as plain, pale, and out of his league. Christian always lets Ana know how beautiful and strong she is ("You are one exquisite woman, Miss Steele!") and she does the same for him. Although he seems to be the perfect man on the outside, his therapist, Dr. Flynn, tells Ana that Christian has "morbid self-abhorrence." He suffers from a low self-image, does not feel deserving, and he thinks of himself as broken. She continually empowers him to see his own beautify and worth.

9. **Communicating intimately with the loved one.** Ana is processing every aspect of the relationship as they go along and she is big on communicating. Christian has secrets and he tends to withhold them and not say much unless pressed — until midway through book two when he begins to really share. In real relationship time, it is only about three weeks or so from their first meeting to the time he opens up to her and shares many of his demons. From there the communication becomes a regular feature.

10. **Valuing the loved one.** These characters truly value and respect each other. It is a very appealing relationship because you sense the depth of their trust and connection. Christian often says to Ana, "Do you know how much you mean to me?" He shows her every day by taking care of her in all ways – even when she resists. She shows through her love. This is corny, but a famous quote from the third book in the trilogy, *Fifty Shades Freed*: "Christian, you are the state lottery, the cure for cancer, and the three wishes from Aladdin's lamp all rolled into one." They admire each other. Christian said he bought the publishing company Ana was working at not to control her career, but with the idea that she would take it over and run it in a year hence. When she protests he proclaims she will be great and that he had his first company at the same age. He truly valued her and knew she was capable.

Passion. It is obvious that Christian and Ana share a great passion with and for each other. Critics say that Ana was crazy to get involved with Christian — because of his penchant for spankings, handcuffs, and the BDSM lifestyle. But that becomes secondary to the deep passion they have for each other. He begins to let go of his need to "punish" her, and she begins to enjoy some of his surprises in what he calls the "Play Room." As Sternberg explains, the passion component of love involves a "state of intense longing for union with the other" (Sternberg, 1999, p. 9). This is something that Christian and Ana express strongly and with great regularity. Their passion is a legend in its own time, and has been helping reader's fuel their own passion. In *Psychology Today,* sex therapist Sari Cooper wrote in March 2012 that the books have opened a new sexual conversation between couples. "Just because the book has become a hit in the suburbs, does not mean that all these female readers want to enact these roles," she writes. "Some will, and some won't." Yet she confirms many couples are seeing bedroom revivals through communication, anticipation, and psychological engagement inspired by *Fifty Shades of Grey*.

Decision and Commitment. Sternberg says this has two components: "The short term aspect is the decision to love a certain other, whereas the long term one is the commitment to maintain the love" (Sternberg, 1999, p. 11). This is an interesting aspect for Christian and Ana. Like in many new relationships, it *seemed* to take a while before anyone admitted loving the other however, since the relationship took off so quickly the declarations of love came after just a few weeks.

Because the book is from the heroine's point of view we hear her decision of love before his. Christian's confessions of love begin like more of surrender to some unfathomable, mystical power she has over him. "'What the hell are you doing to me?'" he breathes as he nuzzles my neck. "'You completely beguile me, Ana. You weave some powerful magic'" (James, 2012, p. 372).

He began the relationship wanting to make her his submissive, and, within a month, he wants to make her his wife. "You are so precious to me Ana. I was serious about marriage. We can get to know each other then. I can look after you. You can look after me. We can have kids if you want. I will lay my world at your feet, Anastasia. I want you, body and soul, forever. Please think about it." Of course, he formally gets down on one knee, surrounded by flowers, and says: "Anastasia Steele. I love you. I want to love, cherish, and protect you for the rest of my life. Be mine. Always, share my life with me. Marry me."

Ana thought long and hard before jumping in because she had a lot to weigh. In the end she decided that although he was complex and difficult, her love for him was stronger.

Fans would agree their decision to stick together came from sheer love. At first, they held on because they were afraid of losing each other and then they began to truly build a life together. It is Ana's words of love that close the trilogy, "Life is never going to be boring with Christian, and I'm in this for the long haul," writes E. L. James on the final page of *Fifty Shades Freed*. "I love this man: my husband, my lover, father of my child, my sometimes dominant ... my Fifty Shades."

Part Three

Interviews with Experts and Fans

Chapter 15

Why Mr. Grey's Dominance is Such a Turn On
Interview with Stephen Snyder, M.D.

Christian Grey's pure mastery in the bedroom, the Red Room, and beyond is a great turn on. Readers became smitten with the idea of having someone with such expertise, who knows what to do, where to touch, etc. Stephen Snyder M.D., a New York City sex therapist who has been following the *Fifty Shades* trend since it began, says there are certain qualities that Christian brings to the party.

"Christian Grey is a fictionalized sexual dominant (Dom)," he said. "To be a Dom, you have to do the following things that women generally appreciate." He offers these insights:

1. **You have to be sincerely interested in sex.**

   That doesn't sound too hard, right? Aren't all guys interested in sex? Actually, no. Not from a woman's point of view. You take a woman out on a date, you can be sure that her hair, her skin, her outfit, even her shoes have all been studied very carefully. Christian Grey sweats the details in just that way. His clothes, his body-wash, the music in his car. He's interested in the whole sensory experience. Just like most women. Christian Grey is so interested in sex that he has a whole room devoted to it. OK, it's full of implements of pain, but he keeps it all very organized and in good repair, even during the NFL playoff season. Sex is his biggest priority. How many men can honestly say that?

2. **You really have to pay attention.**

   In a sexual encounter, Ana has Christian's complete attention. That's a *big* turn-on to most women. A Dom has to have done considerable research about what turns on his submissive (sub), and what doesn't. He has to know her needs and her limitations. A good Dom doesn't have to keep being reminded not to bite his sub's nipples too hard. He takes responsibility for remembering. Many married women start to feel like their husband's mother when they have to keep reminding him of these things. With a good Dom, that doesn't happen.

3. **You have to know how to be a leader.**

   Sex is like dancing. A man's got to know how to lead. Most ordinary women are exhausted from thinking so much all the time. They appreciate a chance to let someone else do the planning. Each time Christian Grey takes Ana into his secret sex room, he's got the agenda figured out in advance. He doesn't have to ask her whether she's seen his mid-sized anal beads lying around. She can just relax, listen to the sensuous music on his sound system, and surrender.

Christian Grey entices women into a fantasy world that touches them on all cylinders and may have helped pep things up in the bedroom.

The Psychology of Surrender

"A lot of it has to do with what one might call 'the psychology of surrender,'" says Snyder. "Many women enjoy playing with that in fantasy."

"It's well known that *Fifty Shades of Grey* began as a work of 'Fan Fiction' published online, closely based on *Twilight*. *Fifty Shades* is five cups *Twilight*, one cup *Marquis de Sade*, and three cups raw sex. The romantic and erotic ingredients of *Twilight* are closely copied in *Fifty Shades*. Don't be fooled by the fact that *Fifty Shades* is loaded with graphic sex, while the *Twilight* characters never saw each other naked until volume four. It's the same deal."

"Like Edward in *Twilight*, Christian Grey is the epitome of male dominance, with just the right amount of *dangerousness* added. But at the same time he is the best listener in the world. How often do those qualities come together in reality? Grey's scariness, combined with his utter goodness, sincerity, and attention to detail — that's a special formula designed to make women want to buy more books and see the movie too!"

Chapter 16

Why Are Fans Are So Attached to Christian Grey?
Interview with Barna William Donovan, Ph.D.

Why are we so attached to our favorite fictional characters, and, specifically, Mr. Christian Grey?

I spoke to Barna William Donovan, Ph.D., of the Department of Communication at Saint Peter's University in Jersey City, N.J., and an expert on fan behavior, about why we get so involved with favorite fictional characters and how it can lead to strong public reactions to movie casting decisions.

"The Internet has made fandom both more enjoyable and has made fans more powerful," said Dr. Donovan, who is also author of several books on the topic of fandom, including *Blood, Guns, and Testosterone: Action Films, Audiences*, and a *Thirst for Violence and Conspiracy Films: A Tour of Dark Places in the American Conscious*. "Fandom has always been a communal activity. Fans like to get together with other fans and like to discuss the entertainment they love so much. However, the Internet also lets them organize and express their anger when they don't like something about the direction of their favorite entertainment."

Here's our interview on the allure and appeal of Christian Grey, and why we get attached to fictional men:

Why do you think the character of Christian Grey strikes such a chord in women?

Dr. Barna William Donovan: Christian Grey is a safe fantasy of a strong, aggressive, and dangerous lover. There has been a lot of controversy about whether or not this character is really abusive and whether the books are glamorizing an abusive and controlling relationship. But when women read a book, they can safely indulge in a fantasy of danger; they can get a cathartic enjoyment out of imagining themselves in a relationship they would probably not want to be in, in real life.

So, we appreciate our Alpha male rule breakers ... from a distance.

In a world that has gotten as politically correct as ours, where culture and entertainment has been pressuring men to tone down the Alpha male aggressiveness for decades now, Christian Grey is a rebel. He breaks the rules and behaves in a way and treats women in a way that men are always told they're not supposed to. Rebellion is always very alluring. Breaking rules and norms and expectations of polite society can be very sexy. When we live in a world where we have so many rules and regulations telling people what they're not supposed to do, trying to control pleasure and trying to tell us how to have fun and how not to have fun, it can be entertaining to read about the kind of character who lives exactly on his own terms.

Is the kind of devotion and obsession we see for Christian Grey anything new?

In romance literature the dangerous leading man who plays by his own rules and aggressively pursues and dominates women has always been very popular. In the classical romance novel, this model of the male hero, in fact, has been the standard. Only for the last decade or so, with the rise of the "chick lit" fiction, about more empowered female characters, has this kind of character declined somewhat in popularity. But that might be the very reason for Christian Grey's success now. He merely reaffirms the attractiveness of danger and rebellion.

It seems like ancient history now, but wasn't there a similar fan excitement for the character of Edward Cullen in *Twilight*?

Yes, I think the two characters are very similar, although aimed at different audiences. They are both strong and potentially aggressive. Since the *Twilight* books are aimed at a younger audience, largely the young adult audience and even the teen audience, those books highlight Edward's "potential" danger. He's a good vampire who tries to control his domineering and deadly impulses around the girl he loves, but the danger is still there, lurking beneath the surface.

Why do think readers get so attached to WHO will portray their favorite characters?

When someone reads a book, they become the director of the movie version of the book playing out in their heads. They imagine who would be so perfectly cast as a character. But when the actual movie comes along, the real thing shatters the fantasy in the mind of the fan. This can be very frustrating if the actual cast is radically different from what the reader imagined in her mind for such a long time.

How would you explain the "personal" relationship we have with our favorite character?

The relationship we have with our favorite character is always one where the fictional character in some way reflects values that we already have. This is why I don't think the relationship is as simple as a powerful media inspiring people to become obsessed fans. People become obsessed fans of certain types of characters they feel reflect values they already have. For example, *Star Trek* fans say they already have certain beliefs about what the future should look like and how people should live together. *Star Trek* merely came along and happened to have the same sort of values that a big enough sector of the audience already had. It's the same way with *Fifty Shades of Grey*. I believe that the connection between the avid fan and Christian Grey is this same kind of fulfillment of an already existing wish. There are some women who already find a Christian Grey-type character attractive or find his qualities important in a man and now they will become fans of this particular series of books because they speak to the fan's existing values.

What are some of the good things Christian Grey has done for readers, couples, and making sex a little more fun?

I think the good thing these books and Christian Grey have done — and why I am glad to see the runaway success of the *Fifty Shades* books — is that they confirmed that sexual fantasy, role-playing, and experimentation are all normal and healthy parts of sexuality. Even with the BDSM aspect of these books, the stories are about a consensual relationship and characters freely exploring what brings them pleasure. American society and popular culture have long had an incredibly split attitude toward sex. On the one hand, sexual imagery is ubiquitous in all of the mass media, used to sell just about everything, but, on the other hand, open and public acknowledgements of the complexities of sexual pleasure and sexual health are still controversial topics. I like the fact that so many women are not ashamed to admit that they love these books and that they feel it is empowering and normal to pursue sexual fantasies. The popularity of *Fifty Shades* merely lets us as a society openly discuss how we all are complex sexual beings and the pursuit of sex and the indulgence in fantasy in a consensual relationship is nothing dirty or improper.

Chapter 17

A Greater Understanding of the BDSM Lifestyle and a Needed Conversation About the Difference Between Abuse and BDSM

Psychologist Alexis Conason, Psy.D, a researcher at St. Luke's-Roosevelt Hospital in New York City and in private practice, specializes in treatment of body image and sexual issues. She says there may be elements of abuse in the relationship between Anastasia Steele and Christian Grey depicted in *Fifty Shades of Grey* but that it is important to differentiate between the BDSM relationship and emotional or physical abuse.

"BDSM is characterized by a safe and playful arrangement between two consenting adult partners," she said. "Before entering into a BDSM relationship, partners should clearly define the boundaries of what they and their partner want and are willing to engage in. BDSM does not involve emotional or physical abuse. Emotional and/or physical abuse is no more common in BDSM relationships than in "vanilla" or any other type of relationships. A common myth about BDSM is that it is associated with a history of sexual abuse. This is a myth perpetuated in *Fifty Shades* by Christian's disclosure of his sexual abuse history. Most people who engage in BDSM do so because they enjoy it and it is fun and pleasurable for them, not because they are acting out a pattern of abuse."

Abuse is in the Eyes of Beholder

Although Christian begins his journey with Ana in a harsher manner, true blue fans who've read the full trilogy know that he healed and transformed. Many do not consider his actions abusive; or, they feel he was redeemed in his willingness to change for the woman he loved.

"Everything in the book is safe, sane and consensual," says Jamie Turner, of South Carolina, a married mom of one who is the executive director of a local non-profit organization. She's read the trilogy four times. "Ana did nothing against her will. She questioned. They communicated. Different from the mainstream view of sex, yes. Abusive, no."

"Nothing about the books seemed harmful or violent to me," she says. "The spanking at the end of the first book was tough to read, but because of the ramifications, both characters were open to change, healing and love. What great love story doesn't have a little pain and heartache? This one is no different."

"I love the changes that Christian and Ana's love brought to their lives," says Turner. "I especially love the change in Christian. He went from a hurt, isolated man who felt completely unworthy of love to a passionate, loving, warm man who was brave enough to let Ana into his heart. They both grew, and it took the love and acceptance from each other to do so. Ana truly stepped into Christian's darkness and brought him out into the light. We should all be so lucky to love and be loved as deeply."

Angela Bray, a medical coder and biller in Kentucky, who is happily married with two kids, agrees. She has read the trilogy five times.

"If you pay attention to the books you know that Anastasia doesn't do anything that makes her feel uncomfortable or scared and Christian never forces her to do anything she doesn't want to do … even going as far as to ask her what her 'hard limits' are," she says.

Fifty Shades Is Meant to be a Fantasy

Members of the BDSM community do not wax as positively about the books, and they stress that this kind of relationship is not to be taken lightly or handled disrespectfully, but some can see how the books touch a nerve, according to a BDSM practitioner and talk show host known only as Master Jeff. He's co-host of the web series "No Vanilla," on The Experience Channel, with his wife Kelley, who is a submissive.

He said that the BDSM community has concern about the way abuse issues have been tied in with BDSM practices and assessed that the book did not portray a real BDSM relationship. But he also says it is important to remember that the book is supposed to be a fantasy – not a training manual.

"The biggest fantasy for women by far, in several different surveys, has to do with a man that just won't take no for an answer," he said. "Now of course they don't want to take threat into the real world and be threatened or want physical harm to come. But women want to be desired."

This could be why so many women read the trilogy over and over again. They love reliving the intensity of Christian Grey's love and devotion.

"I love how much he loves her (though it takes him a while to admit it)," says Bray. "He is obsessed with her, not in a weird creepy way, but in a way that makes the reader wish they were her. Here is a man who can have any woman he wants and he chose Anastasia Steele. I think the average woman reading this book might be able to imagine herself finding her own Christian Grey."

It's All About Communication

The books have created an invitation to fantasize, to admit fantasies that may have once been consider unacceptable or weird, and even to try some on for size.

"The major pro of *Fifty Shades of Grey* is that it has opened up the discussion of sex and given people permission to try out new sexual activities," says psychologist Conason. "Many couples have difficulties talking directly about sex and the book gave people the opportunity to say: "Honey, check out this passage. That might be fun!"

"The book became such a phenomenon that *everyone* was reading it and so many people were getting turned on by it that it became a social norm," she said. "Women (and men) started to think: if all of these people are turned on by this, maybe it is okay that I like it too. And this opened up opportunities for sexual exploration. I think that anything that opens up sexual exploration without attached guilt and shame is really a wonderful thing."

Chapter 18

Psychologists Say Erotic Books Like 'Fifty Shades' Can Be Good for Us

Although erotic romance books have been around for a long time, they seem to have experienced an amazing resurgence since *Fifty Shades of Grey*. On the bestseller list since 2012, the book has certainly helped open the door to more mainstream acceptance, as well as to sexual curiosity, exploration, and arousal without apology.

Erotic romances can help you explore your fantasies, stimulate your libido, and bring you closer to the one you love, according to the three psychologists I interviewed. Even though these books may be a little addictive, they can be positive for your emotional health and your love life.

They Offer Fun, Fantasy, and Exploration

"The benefits of erotic romances can be fun and entertaining to read, encourage fantasy, and encourage explorations of new sexual activities in a safe way. These may be activities that you do or don't want to try in real life, or may not have the opportunity to try in real life. Do erotic romances create false expectations of men? Perhaps. But no more so than Disney, *Jerry Maguire* (since when do we need someone else to complete us?), or just about any romantic comedy ever made. If you are someone who left *Mr. and Mrs. Smith* feeling despondent that you are not married to Brad Pitt or left *Harry Potter* looking for your magic wand, then yes, you may want to exercise caution when reading erotic romances. However, for most people, erotic romance novels are fiction and can be used as wonderfully sexually stimulating tools for fantasy."

—*Alexis Conason, Psy.D., Licensed Psychologist*

They Are Great Aphrodisiacs

"Erotic romances are an important way to get in touch with your romantic feelings and sexual fantasies. They are a way to develop those fantasies, to better understand what you need, what turns you on, and what helps you feel very intimately connected with your partner. Erotic romances can be great aphrodisiacs, and truly a benefit to relationships. Or they can be a fulfillment in themselves and a detriment to your relationship. Isn't this true of so many things in life? If you can bring it home and share it, it's great. But if you escape into it, and meet your needs in a more solitary and self-absorbed way, it can become a problem or worsen existing problems. We want to feel the heat! But the important thing is to take that home, talk about them, enact them, experiment, and be freer as a couple."

-*Carl G. Hindy, Ph.D. Licensed Clinical Psychologist*

They Help You Accept Love

"There are multiple benefits to erotic reading material. Specifically for those that are uncomfortable with intimacy or their sexuality, reading erotic romances can increase comfort. For couples that have problems with differing sex drives, I recommend reading these novels as foreplay or a way to increase desire. Additionally, these novels often describe relationships between individuals that learn to accept the love of another and be vulnerable. This is modeling positive outcomes for individuals that struggle with allowing themselves to be open and vulnerable in relationships."

-Nerina Garcia-Arcement, Ph.D., Licensed Clinical Psychologist

Part Four

E.L. James Opened a
New Door to Erotic Romance
Now Every One is Reading —
and Writing — Them!

Chapter 19

14 Top Authors on Steamy Perks of Reading and Writing Sexy Romances

When I wrote my first steamy erotic romance novel over twenty years ago, it was sold in the secret back section of book stores, sex novelty shops, or by mail order — and shipped in a plain brown wrapper. Oh my, how things have changed!

Although erotic romance books have been around for a long time, they seem to have experienced an amazing resurgence since *Fifty Shades of Grey*.

Today, women are proud devotees of sexy, red-hot romance stories and they adore the authors who spin tales of hot Alpha men who know how to please a woman from head to toe. Anyone who has spent time on Facebook pages devoted to authors and book boyfriends knows the days of blushing over sex scenes is a thing of the past. Fans, these days, are quite forthright about their enjoyment of erotic encounters between their favorite fictional couples.

For my "Hot Romance" column in *The Three Tomatoes,* I reached out to many of today's most popular bestselling authors of steamy romances and asked them to share their thoughts on why these books are great for readers and their relationships, and how beneficial it is to see erotic love stories embraced as part of the mainstream.

"I think the widespread acceptance of erotic romance — thank you E.L. James — combined with the widespread availability of e-readers are like a perfect storm that has caused this newfound sexual revolution of sorts," says K. Bromberg, author of the bestselling *Driven* series.

"Women are no longer embarrassed to talk to other women about sex," Bromberg says. "Women are now reading these scenes in explicit detail, becoming comfortable with the terms and new ideas, and then suggesting them to their partners. What better way to spice up your relationship that has turned predictable over time than to try new things? The mere fact that women realize they can be classy and modest as they were always taught they needed to be, and at the same time be little vixens in the sack is extremely empowering to the woman herself and to the gender as a whole. This genre has given women confidence, a newfound sense of self, and allowed them to read about fantasies they once might have thought about but never dared to ask their significant others to try. Now, they are reading a scene, seeing it play out, and then figuring out for themselves if it really is something they want to try. How cool is that?"

Here are what some of the other top-selling authors had to say:

"Erotic romance has been around for a long time, but I think you're right in that it's been in the past few years that it's become less taboo for readers to admit they enjoy the genre. I think romance novels have been popular for so many years because they feed a woman's need for fantasy and romance. It sparks her imagination, and it can certainly carry over to her relationships too." **- Kristin Proby**, *With Me In Seattle Series*

"I think anything that encourages a woman to embrace her sexuality is a good thing. Romance books, and especially erotic romances, have come a long way in the last few years. Women in these books are no longer weak and introverted. They are strong and independent and aren't afraid to explore their bodies and take charge in the bedroom. There's nothing better than getting lost in a book that helps you embrace your inner goddess!" - **Tara Sivec**, *Chocolate Lovers Series*

"Every day Christina and I sit down to write, we work to dispel the idea that romance is about women being self-indulgent. Romance novels allow women to reflect, to escape, to play, to learn. We want women to feel powerful in every facet of their lives, and when we write our erotic romances, we embrace women as strong, opinionated, sexual beings. Women dominate in our ability to create connections, to relate to others, to form communities. It stands to reason that we love books about the fantasy of love, of friendship, of sex. Each of us has our own path in life, with friends and family and lovers, but how much fun is it to read about different experiences? I like to think it's just like my father reading about new civilizations on Mars – a boss falling in love with his headstrong, ambitious intern is a frontier I've personally never explored, but I *love* to think it exists." - **Lauren Billings**, *half of the writing team of* **Christina Lauren**, *The Beautiful Series*

"I have gotten loads of feedback from women telling me how much acting out the scenes from my books has enriched their love lives or how the material has encouraged them to be more creative. And too many times to count, I've gotten messages from women saying their husbands thank me. While that is humorous, it seems that kick-starting the libido with sensual reading can end in some fun time between mates. Pleasurable reading followed by pleasurable exploration. I call that win-win!" - *M. Leighton*, *Bad Boys Series*

"It's spice. It's an escape. It's a fresh perspective on love, on sexuality. Erotic romance, at its best, shows what a good romantic relationship should be: a balanced, erotic partnership, wherein both people seek the pleasure and happiness of the other person as their primary focus." - **Jasinda Wilder**, *Alpha Series*

"I love erotic romance because I think the genre represents freedom for women to experience life and love to the fullest possibilities. It's high time we overcome the expectations of past generations that insist we stay in a box not of our own making." – **Lisa Renee Jones**, *Inside Out Series*

"Erotica empowers women. Erotica shows them that it's acceptable and healthy to take control of their own sexuality. There's no shame in wanting and enjoying sex, even if it's non-Vanilla." - **Denise Grover Swank**, *Rose Gardner Mystery series*

"I love the fact that erotic romance has grown wildly in popularity in the last few years. Not only has it reintroduced many people to the joys of reading, it has also encouraged women to be more open about their sexuality."- **C.C. Wood**, *Girl Next Store Series*

"I believe the steamy romance novel craze has helped women in expressing their own sexual desires to their partners in a healthy way. Reading these novels gives them a sense of empowerment over their own physical needs and allows them to know they aren't alone — that it's okay to want a fulfilling sexual relationship. I can't tell you how many times readers have told me that their husbands thank me. It's nice to know that not only have my stories entertained them, but have improved their quality of life as well." - **Michelle A. Valentine**, *Black Falcon Series*

"I definitely think erotic romances have had a positive effect on women's sexual self-expression. As much as we as a society are trying to make strides to eliminate the negative and derogatory terms used in relation to women and their sexuality, there is still a lot of mixed messages and confusion out there. Hopefully the genre removes that negativity and allows women to feel like they can just be themselves in life and in sex."- **Samantha Young**, *On Dublin Street Series*

"In my opinion, embracing fantasy, especially in books, is important for the simple fact that it allows us to let go of the day-to-day stresses of our regular routine. It offers us an opportunity to get lost in something that could potentially be so far outside of our reality that we may not recognize it, but that doesn't mean we shouldn't experience it. In fact, opening ourselves up to these new things is how we got to where we are today. One of the greatest things that I've heard from readers was that my books help to turn things around in the bedroom. It makes my heart smile to know that not only have they gotten lost in the characters, or enjoyed the story, but they've received something more tangible from the book." - **Nicole Edwards**, *Club Destiny Series*

"Fantasy is a mental vacation. When a woman escapes into a romantic novel, she doesn't just get to be a voyeur she actually gets a chance to mentally morph into a new character. She may be a mother of two with a pile of laundry and a tired husband, but in her latest fictional journey she briefly leaves her ordinary world and gets to be a young socialite, or perhaps a powerful dominatrix, or better yet a naïve virgin catching the attention of a millionaire. We live vicariously through books and get to enjoy many lives without leaving our homes." – **Tali Alexander**, *Love in Rewind*

"It's [erotic romance] the next frontier for feminism. We have broken so many boundaries in the last century or so, but there is still such a stigma regarding sex and women. It's different for men. Women aren't supposed to feel sexy or lose their virginity or want to have a sexual relationship. These books are taking us where our minds and hearts always have been; making it more acceptable and comfortable for us to be the sexual beings we were born to be. I also find that the stories can help strengthen relationships. Women need some downtime and relaxation before getting in the mood. Books can help women do that. Reading and writing them has certainly strengthened my marriage!" - **Laurelin Paige**, *The Fixed Series*

Chapter 20

100 Reasons Why Fans Fell Hard for Fifty

In the past three years I have interacted with thousands of fans, as a fan page administrator and journalist. I polled fans regularly about all things *Fifty* and they shared their opinions generously – a trademark of this fan world!

Once I asked members of the *Fifty Shades of Grey News* page on Facebook what they loved most about the *Fifty Shades* trilogy, and if they liked the books for the romance or the kinky sex. Responses came pouring in from hundreds of fans, and hands down: They loved the love story.

This was before the movie was out, at a time when all they could speak to was the books themselves. This really captures the purity of fan appreciation when the books first landed in our hands and Kindles.

Obviously many of these responses are redundant, but I loved reading them and thought other fans would, too. They are a tiny microcosm but I think they are representative of the gigantic fan base that *Fifty Shades* has reached — and touched.

Since this was a crowdsourced response we have identified the fan only by first name and last initial.

1. It's not about the sex. It's about the love between Christian and Ana, the chemistry and emotion comes over so well on paper. I have never before read a book that has had me so hooked. - Nicci M.

2. It's not just about the BDSM, it's the history Christian has, the chemistry between them both, everything in these books is enthralling, ooh so much love, anger, anguish torment and sexiness. – Pamela P.C.

3. It's about the way he needs her like he needs air. It's about the way that he loves her like there's nothing else in the world. It's how she loves him in spite of him being "fifty shades of fucked up" and how she's willing to try to give him what she thinks he needs. And it's about how he will try "more" for her. – Lori C.

4. It's the relationship. Most men are not romantic. That is what most women want, for a man to take control and to love them the way a man should. – Roxann M.

5. For me, it's not about the sex. It's about the romance. It's the storyline that pulled me in. - Lauren E.

6. Two words: Christian Grey. And I do adore the story. – Christina R.

7. For me this book is my ultimate fantasy! A sexy man commanding me to obey! Yes BDSM is sexy in this type of context! For me it's what I wish I could get from time to time! My husband is more of Mr. Darcy than Mr. Grey. - Nikki D. P.

8. It's not about the bondage for me; it's the romance of Ana and Christian. How this one woman changes everything in his life and he hers. The book is not about bondage; that's just a part

of his life before he meets Ana. And how that life melts away some as he realizes he doesn't need it, but still likes kinky fuckery. – Bethlane K.

9. Most women want a man who's rich, good looking, take-charge, compliments us all the time and aims to please us sexually. - Kasey W.

10. I find the romance a major turn on. The erotica is just the icing on the cake. – Julie W.

11. I think this is one of the most beautiful love stories I have ever read. When I hear someone hasn't read it I say, "You have to read it, it's the best love story ever." I truly believe that! - Melissa B.

12. It's the "power exchange." Most women don't want a wimp, especially in the bedroom. Certainly he (Christian) is a powerful business entrepreneur, but he exudes "power" in every other aspect of his being. She (Anastasia), as well, has the power of a woman's sensuality over him. And "yes" we do like the BDSM part of it, as well. It is very sexy to have a man want YOU that badly. Most of all there's love … and that's an aphrodisiac in and of itself. - Linda K. F.

13. Mr. Grey totally talks my love language. He doesn't say, "I love you" all day long, but does a lot of things to — and for — Ana, that scream: "I LOVE YOU." My kind of guy. – Henriette A.

14. For me it was the story as a whole: The way Christian adores and loves her and lays his world at her feet. He would do anything to make her happy. And in turn she gives him the same. She doesn't give up on him because of his fucked up past. Its unconditional love, which let's face it, we all want and desire.

I think the whirlwind of their romance is just awesome — passion in all aspects. – Heather G.

15. It allows the reader to escape into a world they may otherwise be intimidated by or afraid of. We can escape into the love and internal battling between Christian and Ana without having to endure all the pain (sexual and of the heart) ourselves. I'm a sucker for a love story. I think the world of BDSM is interesting. I may not be personally into but it's interesting, nonetheless. - Chalene R. A.

16. For me it was the almost instant attraction that they had. He treasures her but he doesn't quite know how to show it at first. - Stephanie P. M.

17. For me, the book was brilliantly written. It had all the things a great book needs: good storyline, suspense, well executed and sexy. Now on to the BDSM: I think most woman WANT a man to dominate in the bedroom. This does not have to include bondage and the like, but the majority of us want our men to take charge. BUT, Fifty was more than just that. If you really read the trilogy you will note that Christian lived his life the only way he knew up until he found love. Ana had no clue at all but taught him how to love, properly. If you keep an open mind when you read the trilogy, you will find that it was so much more than just BDSM. Advice to all men, start reading Erotica! You will learn so much and will please your lady likes she's never been pleased! - Trish P. B.

18. Hell Yeah, that is some hot stuff. I personally wouldn't do the "if I don't do as you say you'll be punished stuff," but just the idea of it the fantasy is hot as hell. It's kind of like *Playboy* for men, for us women but it opens your imagination and takes you

out of your comfort zone, which is scary and sexy all at the same time. LOL. - Dawn R. D.B.

19. It's also about the love story. Times have changed but women still want romance. It shows that while sex is important you have to show your love that they are indeed wanted and adored. This man didn't know what that was like till he found "the one." – Tonya A.C.

20. When I read it I did not think I was going to like it. I'm not into that stuff but I fell in love with their love story it was an awesome book. - Ashley W.

21. "With a guy, all they notice is the sex parts, but we girls read the story. Christian opens up to Ana about his life, his struggles and promises her the world, even though we know that's never possible. She never asks him for anything. He does it because he cares. He pays attention enough to know when something is on her mind and he listens to her when she's talking. And they both admit to each other they're not perfect. – Crystal M. P.

22. It's the way he feels for her as well … all of us want someone who feels that strongly for us. It's so powerful! – Jacki W.

23. I hadn't read for years, I read it only because my daughter had bought the books and I wondered what all the fuss was about. So having not read for years I found it seriously hot. I love a billionaire and I loved that he fell in love with a "normal" girl who worked in a DIY store. He loved her so much that to begin with He "changed" for her — i.e. became more vanilla. I really, really loved their emails to each other and how they signed off. Maybe it is a book that just appeals to women more than men. – Jo T. F.

24. Men think it's a porn book but that is so not true because they love each other and Christian is sharing and showing Ana his world. - Pamela C.

25. It's an eye opener ... and after reading ... many more women will be more open to possibilities. - Julie A. S.

26. For me it's the thrill of the beast in the bedroom that knows what he wants and will take charge, but is also romantic and capable of showing love and treating her like his most prized possession. It was thrilling and romantic and passionate and an escape from reality. I think that's what drew me in so deeply. – Crystal C.

27. For me it's the way that he loves her so much that he is willing to change a big part of who he is to be with her. – Kristin D.

28. It's not the sex, BDSM or other sexual scenes and parts. It's the way Christian is. The love, the romance, the commitment — the way he just is her end-all and be-all. His confidence, sex appeal, the way he just takes control but in an affectionate way. A true love story. - Nazreen K.

29. Every girl likes the thought of being the change in a guy. They both helped each other in different ways to learn and grow. The erotica is second to all that. - Gena S. A.

30. I think these books should come with a warning because your expectations of your partner will hit the roof. LOL. – Tracy C.

31. I just got out of a dysfunctional relationship. For me it's how much he loves her and wants to keep her safe and their magical love for each other gives me hope of "more." – Annie M.

32. It's the intensity of the relationship. There was passion in everything they did together, not just sex. – Cheryl V. L.

33. For me it's a light shone into a world you didn't know you were allowed to like. I mean who would ever imagine Ana in a sexual world like that? She would never, ever consider something like that. That's hot as hell! If you don't like it, it obviously ain't your cup of tea. – Tant T.

34. He makes her feel wanted and all women want that feeling. - Tiffany B.

35. Well, for me it had nothing to do about BDSM. I found it to be a love story, about a man who in so many ways was a child and found a woman who at the end was just more than sex. I love a man that protects a woman, who sits by her bedside when she's sick or hurt, who buys her a car that's safe to drive, etc. That's what I love about Fifty! – Lori K. M.

36. It is not about the sex. It is the love story. I do not know a person alive that does not want someone to love them the depth that they LOVE each other. It is an amazing love that I had at one time and it was taken away! – Kerry S. H.

37. Deep down every woman is either a little freak or a whole lotta freak! Men have NO clue what women want. Maybe if they treated women the way CG does in this book more women would be open to the idea of opening up that side! Most men just want the down and dirty without the sensitive, and this book is what most women want in a man! All a woman wants is a man to be her everything! – Glynn A. S.

38. Great love story and any girl would want a little bit of this kind of life. Admit it or not! But it's just that … fantasy. Nothing wrong with getting lost in it every now and then. – Donna P.

39. In all of the ties and kinky fuckery he STILL WAS A GENTLEMAN to her! Men lack that part! – Glynn A. S.

40. Some women like the idea of it and would secretly like to try some of the things in the book but don't have the courage to do it. We women are all different but deep down we want the same things. - Helen B.

41. It wasn't your "mothers romance novel!" It was more "up to the times." The BDSM? Not into that as a personal activity, but reading someone's thoughts (as the book states) can be entertaining, funny and sexual. For some, a little role play/domination can be exciting behind closed doors. There was more to the story than just the sex, though, and you get wrapped up into the character's story/life. Once you become attached to them and maybe even relate to them in some way, it keeps your interest peaked. Sure, some things were just not likely to ever happen, but it was still good reading. He had a past that he didn't want to share … as many people have a past that they don't want to share. Ana broke Christian from his normal pattern of behavior and rocked his world — in ways other than just sex. – Rachel H.

42. Everyone who hasn't read the book just thinks it's this kinky sex novel that we women are lusting over! This couldn't be more incorrect. While the sex scenes are quite risqué and exciting, the sex isn't what sucked me in. The love story beyond all the sex is phenomenal! She takes this broken man and makes him open up to love and a relationship; he turns her from this shy little

girl into this beautiful woman willing to explore her boundaries! – Mandy F. M.

43. What I love about the book is everything. How the "ugly duckling" if you will, is the star here. I get so tired of it always being the "hot chick" I'm just an average girl. And it's nice for the average girl to finally be wanted. And not only is she wanted, it's in such an intense and extraordinary way! I would absolutely LOVE to feel someone want me so badly — Red Room or no. Although the BDSM is pretty hot! - Heidi S. S.

44. It's about the intensity of it. The whole package. He is everything all wrapped into one and we want all of it. – Rene L. B.

45. I was drawn into the book because of the caring emotional commitment that joined the characters together. - Judy T. K.

46. It's the Cinderella story aspect of it. – Rhonda C.

47. For most women it isn't the BDSM. It is a little exciting in a way, like watching through a sheer curtain into the BDSM world. For me it was the fact that a man was able to take a look at his life and finally face his demons of his past. To see what is in front of him. The idea that a man would do something so hard to be with a woman he loves, the first woman he has ever loved. We are drawn to the love aspect. That knock you on your knees, can't eat, can't sleep, one in a million, no one else has this love. Which in human nature is what we all truly want. Plus the panty dropping sexy millionaire who can make you cream yourself just by looking at you. - Deja F.

48. It creates the illusion that every woman desires … a man that loves her so deeply, he changes. - Courtney K.

49. Because Christian is the guy that we all want — a true love, a dominant man, and one hell of a provider. – Dawn D. B.

50. Great love story. Opposites really do get together. – Heather P. C.

51. It has the romance that women love and need, and enough porn for us to be comfortable. For some of us the man is controlling enough to make us feel safe but the woman has enough control to keep him in check. And of course, it has the happily ever after that we all like to believe in. - Launa R. O.

52. It's a love story first and foremost to me. It's about a tortured young man who despite his best efforts not to, falls in love and he fights it all the way. When he realizes, it's a beautiful thing. I just love it and I love Christian. – Kelly D.

53. First, the story of how a guy who has everything fell in love with a girl who's ordinary makes it extraordinary! Second, the guy, Christian Grey, is perfect in everything and he's a kind of man that every girl dreamed of, so of course it would attract girls' attention. Third, it's more than a love story but it also tells that love can bring the best in you and from the story we could see how much Christian and Ana changed each other for the better. And about the BDSM? I think it is just kind of a background to make the character of Christian Grey more interesting. I think it means that everyone has their own secrets and BDSM is Christian's. I don't really care about the BDSM since I'm only interested in him.

In my opinion, I think people really need to see the story from the positive side too not only from the negative side. - Lalanti N.

54. I love the book because it shows how women should be treated. I don't mean about the BDSM things … I mean how Christian loves Ana. It is just how it should be to all of us also. He made Ana feel that she is beautiful in every way and that she is the most important to him even forsaking others. He helped develop her self-esteem and self-worth and she taught him how to trust. For me it is a great love story more than anything! I truly wish to meet the Christian Grey of my life! - MamaNi B.

55. Everyone has different reason for liking the books. For some it's the love story, for others the sexual fantasy, for me it's all of the above. He pushes her to live out her desire and fantasy and not to be afraid. It's girl porn, LOL. It's the love with the sex – not just the, "let's get naked and f***k" kinda sex guys are used to; it's deeper than that. - Maryann R.

56. It's the passion in the book that I love! - Tone S. S.

57. 21st century love story with a hint of spice! – Timea K. G.

58. Love, passion and the loss of control. Giving everything to one person completely. – Kimberly S.

59. One of the best series I ever read and not for the sex and BDSM parts — even though they were HOT. This is the ultimate love story … two people who love each other unconditionally and can just be themselves around each other. – Jessica J.

60. Let's call it what it is … a grown up Cinderella story! Young woman from meager beginnings with self-confidence issues meets attractive man with money, smarts, culture and power. He spoils her with things she cannot afford to do for herself, gives her mind-blowing orgasms and super-hot intense sex! All while falling in love with each other and building a deep

emotional and romantic relationship. What's not to like? – Jennifer M. G.

61. It's the way he looks at her like no one else exist. How he gave her confidence in herself. She will go to any measure to please him and he pleases her — he changes his whole life just for her. – Ashley A.

62. It's the fantasy of a man like CG wanting a good, down to earth, normal woman! We all like a "Take Control Kinda Guy" but can stand on our own two feet! A *Pretty Woman* scenario, without the prostitution! - Heather H. C.

63. Because it's sexy! – Sabrina S.

64. It's more than sex. It's the love that grows between two people and how they help each other grow. – Lori R.

65. For myself and most women I know that have read these books (multiple times for most of us) it really has little if anything to do with the BDSM … it's all about the romance … how they both changed … met each other half way … the way all relationships should be. – Maura N. L.

66. If men read these books … all women's sex lives would improve — because women want to be satisfied! But I think it's mainly how he surprises her and treats her, just sexy in general. – Shannon K.

67. It's the way he loves her! – Rayetta L. L.

68. Their willingness to struggle and compromise to meet each other's needs … because they love their partner. To overcome demons of the past and let go of preconceived ideas — because they so much love the other person. – Margaret B

69. My husband asks the same question all the time. I've read excerpts from the books to him — kinky and not — and he still doesn't get it. I think the best way to describe why we love it so much is the actual love story! Because believe it or not, it really is about a love story and how her love for him changes who he wants/needs to be. He becomes her everything. Yes, all the "kinky fuckery" helps spice it up, because let's be honest, their story drags on and on and on throughout all three books. – Harmoney J. W.

70. If I want romance I'll read Harlequin ... it's about the SEX!! Let's just be honest! Passion, intensity, chemistry, and freakilicious! - Rhonda P. B.

71. It's not about Dom to sub. It's about a girl who has never really loved, loving this severely messed up guy, who is willing to give up all he knows for her. – Lori H.

72. I love the love story part in the book. I sometimes skipped the BDSM parts. – Jaline S.

73. It's not the BDSM. It's finding someone that you can lose yourself in, someone you feel safe enough to be able to lose control with. It's that someone that worships you. The hot sex is ok too. – Melissa S.

74. I don't see the whole crazy sex they have. What made me more curious was to see why he was the way he was, plus the love that blossomed between the two! – Crystal G.L.

75. It's about a man who can take control and be sensitive and gentle. And about someone loving and wanting you so very deeply! – Cherie M.

76. I personally read and love this trilogy because of the excitement: the suspense of the events as well as the "fairy tale" way Christian would die and lives for "his Ana." Every woman wants the romance and undying love whether she admits it or not. – Chastity U. W.

77. I love the romantic side! Every time I read it I skip the sex parts now. I enjoy the love. – Amiee C. M.

78. I think nearly every woman would want a fella that's so in love and treats her like she's a princess. And the connection between them, it's like they can overcome anything if they are together. It's sweet as well as sexy. – Chloe B.

79. It's the love story and how he changed his whole world for just an ordinary girl who fell into his office. - Lindsay H. C.

80. I fell in love with this book because of how it changed both of the characters' lives by finding each other and falling in love in the process. As for the BDSM, it is about trust. You'd be surprised how many women are submissive as much as dominant. It's not about hurting or degrading your sub. You have to understand the concept of BDSM to fully appreciate it. But it's not for everyone. You have to have open mind. - April A. L.

81. Plain and simple underneath all the SEX there really is a love story under there. - Charlene L.

82. For me I found it to be a "true love story" it showed what happened to make him the way he was, what things she was willing to do and change because of her love for him and how that love "fixed" what was "wrong" with him. How it helped him to love himself. It wasn"t really about the sex for me - it was about true unconditional love. – Debbie B. D.

83. CTG is just an amazing man in the books — his love for Ana and what lengths he goes through to protect her. He treats her like a Queen. What woman wouldn't want a man like that? – Terri R. W.

84. Every woman wants a man that will fight for her in every way possible. - Kathy E.

85. In my opinion it's not about the BDSM. I can do without it in the book. It just makes the book stand out in a way. But for me it's about the romance, and how someone can be so oblivious on how to actually love a woman and yet fall full heartedly. And for a woman to love him so much she is willing to help him in his hard times. Christian has great qualities that all women can love. He knows what he wants, he's honest about it, and he takes charge in the bedroom (and that's always sexy). The fact that he's competent is always good and him being rich is just the cherry on the Sunday. – Prisilla O.

86. It's because men like him are so rare. To love someone and actually never take her for granted. Men like that don't really exist in real life. – Rachel P.B.

87. For me it was the love story and the coming to life of Christian — and the kinky fuckery was good too. - Sally S.

88. Oh come on girls we all know it's because of the things he does in bed! We wish our men did those things too — lol. - Jamie S. C.

89. For me it's not about the sex parts, yeah they're a bonus but for me it's listening, how he falls in love with her, and the adventure they go on together — finding out who he is! It's not your typical romance book but I love it! - Natalie R. H.

90. It also showed how a special person can come into your life and turn it upside down, or should I say make it right. It was how they learned to love each other even with all the baggage. I guess most of us women fantasize about meeting a man like him. Someone who you can teach to love, who would want you so much, and who would fulfill all your sexual desires on top of everything else. The perfect love story … only wish it was mine! – Sharon W.

91. The LOVE story!!! The sex is just a bonus! - Tamara J. R.

92. A man that will do anything to please and protect and take care of his woman, and the love that grows between them! What's not to love? – Meri S. P.

93. It's not about the BDSM at all for me. That didn't even have to be in the books! It was about a guy who was lost and the only way he dealt with was the hard core BDMS! And a girl that never thought she was pretty and always hid in life! They found each other and good things happen for the both of them. They found their real selves and a love that is so strong and lasting! Yes and they do have a hot steamy sex life!!! (What is wrong with having hot sex with the one you love?) The beating and the hard-core sex he did was when he was missing something! Most of the sex was just really mind blowing! The worst he did was bust her ass hard and she didn't allow him to get away with it! They are great books when I can see the love that comes from them! The books are about love and the hot sex is just a really good treat to add to the books!!! - Crystal R.

94. It's a story about a girl getting the guy that no girl can get, and a guy opening up. – Samantha S. M.

95. It's more than BDSM, it's a love story, two people fall in love and grow for the better with each other and face things; things they never would have without the other. I love how it shows that she is just as crazy in love with him as he is her and that they're so into pleasing one another. - Alexandrea M.

96. The sex was the least of it. It was the redemption of Christian. Him beating back his demons. Her unconditional love. His wanting to protect her. Sex had nothing to do with it for me as far as loving this LOVE story. - Susan S. M.

97. Women want to feel DESIRED! Women want a man to be so taken by them they can't wait to get their hands on them! Women want a man who sweeps them off their feet, one who finds pleasure in bringing them pleasure. And mostly we just want to feel WANTED and LOVED. We want intensity, passion, and thoughtfulness. – Nychelle H.

98. Don't get me wrong the sex was HOT! But the thing I loved most was his love for her and his willingness to change for her to be a better man. This is the first book that I have read like this but let me assure you it won't be the last! – Jessica W. K.

99. For me it was all of it: The BDSM. The love story. The give-and-take in the relationship. For me this was the total package. Undying love but not in the happily ever after kind of way. They had to fight for their relationship, sometimes their own personal demons. It was a perfect mix of, fantasy, real life, and hot mind blowing sexual encounters. I fell in love with Christian and Ana. – Jamie H. C.

100. "All of the above" - Deena L.

Chapter 21

What She Said:
Author E.L James On Why
Women Love Christian Grey

For over three years I asked fans, authors, psychologists, brain science experts and others why women went so ga-ga over Christian Grey.

Finally, I had the chance to pose the question to author E. J. James when I attended Christian Grey's official Birthday party on Long Island on June 18, 2015, for the launch of *Grey*.

Christian was feted with gray cake and other goodies and the event was covered by the *Today Show*. Participants were asked to write their questions on a card.

It was *Today Show* correspondent, Erica Hill, who brought my question to the author and it ended up on national TV. Needless to say, E. L. James' answer brought roars of laughter from the 350 guests, and probably the national viewing audience!

Erica Hill to E.L. James: **Why do you think we love Christian Grey so much?**

E.L. James: "Because he doesn't exist, really... Christian is a fantasy figure of how we think we want men to be. But, really, we want men to do the washing up!"

You can see the *Today Show* segment here.

https://www.today.com/popculture/fifty-shades-book-grey-celebrated-fans-el-james-today-show-t26996

During the book signing portion of the evening, I had a chance to thank E.L. James and tell her I could now rest my research on the topic as she has finally set the record straight in just a few words!

She was gracious and kind.

In Summary

I poked into the psychological nooks and crannies of the trilogy and probed the fan base for answers, but I did not find a secret magic recipe to explain exactly how *Fifty* had its way with us. But I did identify many magical aspects of the book that helped to make it so special.

I finally got to put the question to the author, and she laughed and gave a funny response. So there is always the chance that I got a little carried away in taking this research so seriously!

But I am glad I gave it a try. And that I shared my findings (and enthusiasm) in my final paper, articles, social media, and this little book. I had lots of fun along the way!

As mentioned before, E.L. James was masterful in her use of erotic cues, and storytelling that stimulates all the senses. And in bringing to life two memorable characters who shared a powerful, transformative love. She's touched fans in a profound way. She also got people reading and writing again, and gave the publishing industry a much needed boost of excitement.

She is also funny as heck, and brought so much of her humor into the book, lightening up a sometimes dark story.

I remain a huge fan of hers for opening the door to a brave new world where women of all ages can enjoy sharing their fantasies, reading hot love stories, and writing erotic romances without shame.

In the process of celebrating *Fifty Shades of Grey* I tapped into my own inner sex goddess and found the courage to write steamy fiction again. I am grateful.

References and Works Cited

Ben-Ze'ev, A. (2004). *Love Online: Emotions on the Internet* (1st ed.). Cambridge, United Kingdom: Cambridge University Press.

Bosman, J. (2014, February 26). For 'Fifty Shades of Grey,' More Than 100 Million Sold. Retrieved November 16, 2015, from http://www.nytimes.com/2014/02/27/business/media/for-fifty-shades-of-grey-more-than-100-million-sold.html

Bradbury, T., & Karney, B. (2010). *Intimate Relationships* (1st ed.). New York, New York: W.W. Norton & Company.

Clarke, B. (2012, September 6). Beauty Myth Author Naomi Wolf Says Women's Badness is Sexual. *Herald Sun*. Retrieved September 6, 2012, from http://www.heraldsun.com.au/entertainment/arts-books/the-beauty-myth-author-naomi-wolf-says-womens-badness-is-sexual-in-her-new-book-vagina-a-new-biography/story-fn7euh6j-1226466553477

Cooper, LCSW, S. (Producer/lecturer) (2012, July 12). Fifty Shades of Grey: What You Can Learn about Sex Esteem from the Bestseller. *Washington Square Institute, New York City.*

Cooper, LCSW, S. (2012, March 6). BDSM: Fifty Shades of Grey Unplugged-Turning up the heat in bedrooms and raising some eyebrows. *Psychology Today*. Retrieved May 6, 2012, from http://www.psychologytoday.com/blog/sex-esteem/201203/bdsm-fifty-shades-grey-unplugged

Conason, PsyD, A. (2012-13) Interviewed in chapter titled "Fifty Shades Has Opened a Greater Understanding of the BDSM Lifestyle" and commented on benefits of erotic romances. Alexis Conason, PsyD is a psychologist, researcher, and author in New York City, reachable at, http://drconason.com/

Donovan, PhD, Barna William, of the Department of Communication at Saint Peter's University in Jersey City, N.J., and an expert on fan behavior. Interviewed on why fans got so attached to who plays Christian Grey. Reachable at http://barnadonovan.blogspot.com/

Falling in love only takes about a fifth of a second, research reveals. (2010, October 22). *Science Daily: News & Articles in Science, Health, Environment & Technology*. Retrieved June 26, 2012, from http://www.sciencedaily.com/releases/2010/10/10102218495 7.htm

Fisher, Ph.D., A., & Costello, V. (2010). *The Chemistry of Love* (1st ed.). New York, New York: Penguin.

Fisher, H. (1992). *Anatomy of Love: A Natural History of Mating, Marriage, and Why We Stray* (1st ed.). New York, New York: Random House.

Fisher, H. (2004). *Why We Love: The Nature and Chemistry of Romantic Love* (1st ed.). New York, New York: St. Martin's Press.

Horstman, J. (2012). *The Scientific American Book of Love, Sex, and the Brain* (1st ed.). San Francisco, California: Jossey-Bass.

James, E. L. (2012). *Fifty Shades Darker: Book Two of the Fifty Shades Trilogy*. (1st ed.). New York, New York: Vintage.

James, E. L. (2012). *Fifty Shades Freed: Book Three of the Fifty Shades Trilogy*. (1st ed.). New York, New York: Vintage.

James, E. L. (2012). *Fifty Shades of Grey: Book One of the Fifty Shades Trilogy.* (1st ed.). New York, New York: Vintage.

Kahn, J. P. (2012). In *Angst: Origins of Anxiety and Depression* (1st ed., pp. 142-143). New York, New York: Oxford University Press.

Kassin, S., Fein, S., & Markus, H. R. (2008). Attraction and Close Relationships. *Social Psychology* (7th ed., pp. 301-343). New York, New York: Houghton Mifflin Company.

Kirshenbaum, S. (2011). *The Science of Kissing* (1st ed.). New York, New York: Grand Central Publishing.

Moberg, K. U. (2003). Oxytocin and Sexuality. In *The Oxytocin Factor: Tapping the Hormone of Calm, Love, And Healing* (1st ed., pp. 118-120). Cambridge, MA: Da Capo Press-Perseus Books Group.

Murphy, A. M. (2012, March 3). Your Brain on Fiction. *The New York Times.* Retrieved July 7, 2012, from http://www.nytimes.com/2012/03/18/opinion/sunday/the-neuroscience-of-your-brain-on-fiction.html?pagewanted=all

Ogas, O., & Gaddam, S. (2011). *A Billion Wicked Thoughts: What the Internet Tells Us About Sexual Relationships* (1st ed.). New York, New York: Plume.

Ortigue, S., Bianchi-Demicheli, F., Frum, C., & Lewis, J. W. (2010). Neuroimaging of Love: MRI Meta-Analysis Evidence toward New Perspectives in Sexual Medicine. *Journal of Sexual Medicine.* doi:10.1111/j.1743-6109.2010.01999.x.

Peele, S. (1988). *The Psychology of Love* (1st ed.). R. J. Sternbery, & M. L. Barnes (Eds.), New Haven, CT: Yale University Press.

Rose, A., & Amen, MD, D. (2014, January 30). 'Fifty Shades of Grey' Is Good For Your Brain, Says Top Doc Daniel Amen. Retrieved November 17, 2015, from http://acroseauthor.com/2014/01/30/fifty-shades-of-grey-is-good-for-your-brain-says-top-doc-daniel-amen/. Interview with Daniel Amen, MD, founder of Amen Clinics, author of over 30 books including *The Brain and Love*.

Rose, A. C. (2015, September 1). The Empowering Perks of Steamy Fiction. *The Three Tomatoes*.

Rose, A. C. (2013, October 18). Why Fans Are So Attached to Christian Grey and Who Plays Him in The 'Fifty Shades' Movie. Retrieved November 16, 2015, from http://acroseauthor.com/2013/10/18/why-fans-are-so-attached-to-christian-grey-and-who-plays-him-in-the-fifty-shades-movie/

Snyder, MD, S. Interviewed for "Why Mr. Grey's Dominance is Such a Turn On." Stephen Synder, MD, is a New York- based sex therapist, who has written extensively on this topic. Available at www.sexualityresource.com

Sternberg, R. J. (1998). *Cupids Arrow: The Course of Love Through Tim* (1st ed.). Cambridge, United Kingdom: Cambridge University Press.

Thornhill, R., Gangestad, S. W., Miller, R., Scheyd, G., McCollough, J. K., & Franklina, M. (2002). Major histocompatibility complex genes, symmetry, and body scent attractiveness in men and women. *Behavioral Ecology, 14*(5), 668-678. Retrieved from http://beheco.oxfordjournals.org/content/14/5/668.full.

Comments from participants of Fifty Shades of Grey News found here:

https://www.facebook.com/FiftyShadesOfGreyFans

Thanks to the Romance Authors Interviewed

My thanks to the authors who commented on the pleasures and power of steamy fiction in our post-Fifty Shades world for an article that first appeared in *Romance at Random*. The article, "The Empowering Perks of Steamy Fiction," is now posted (with links to their books) in my "Hot Romance" column on *The Three Tomatoes*.

If You Haven't Read or Seen Fifty Shades

Fifty Shades trilogy

Grey

Darker

Fifty Shades of Grey movie

Fifty Shades Darker movie

Fifty Shades Freed movie

More From A.C. Rose

AROUSAL

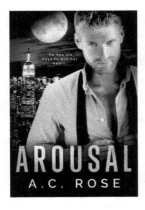

Allison Monroe just got kissed. On an elevator. By a stranger. And she liked it a lot.

But she has no time to be distracted by this gorgeous man, with his panty-melting glances and sexy accent. She's headed to the most important event of her career—a launch party for the new "My Fantasy e-Reader" at Club Kismet, high atop a Manhattan Skyscraper.

She's determined to forget about the amatory elevator ride.

But Nicolai Petre has other ideas. That kiss confirmed what his grandmother's mystical vision had already told him—that Allison is his destiny.

The suave and mysterious European billionaire has six days to win her heart.

This is a super steamy office romance and love story with a unique twist.

DETECTIVE HERCULES

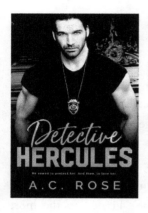

Due to an injury, Detective "Herc" Hercules Andrews is on paperwork detail. He is more than a little bored working the desk in his Manhattan police precinct.

Early one morning he catches a call from a woman with a sultry, sexy voice who needs assistance. Something draws him in. Instead of referring her to 911, he gives her personal attention. He goes way beyond the call of duty when he visits her that night.

Radio dating expert Lizzy Harper shares juicy tidbits from her single-in-the-city life daily on her provocative radio show. She's taken aback by her feelings for the detective who helped her, but she's under pressure to come up with new material. When details of her experience with the hot cop become the talk of her show the following morning, a controversy of epic proportion ensues.

Herc is forced to go undercover—as her boyfriend.

Sparks fly between them, but he discovers Lizzy has more than just fans. There's a menace in their midst. Can Herc uncover the threat and keep Lizzy safe? Will Herc's attachment to Lizzy become personal and permanent?

MY HOT COP

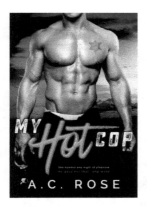

Sometimes the best way to forget about a man who causes you heartache is to find a man who can make you ache with desire.

In this steamy novelette, New York reporter Belle Anderson accepts a weekend assignment in Florida to take her mind off of the handsome surgeon that broke her heart.

She meets hot cop, Lucas Jensen. He's a take-charge, dirty talking Alpha who likes to use his handcuffs for pleasurable pursuits. Lucas agrees to dominate Belle for one night of wild, uncensored passion, with one condition: She must let him take complete command of her body.

Everything the commanding, sexy officer does and says helps heal Belle's heart. But when he asks for more than one night, she wonders if the devoted attention of one powerful man truly help her forget her feelings for another?

This sizzling stand-alone novelette has at HFN ending.

STAY AFTER CLASS

Amanda Slade has a major crush on her sexy art professor and wants his help with an important extracurricular activity: Project VirgEnd.

Professor Jem Nichols knows falling for his beautiful student is a bad idea but he just can't say goodbye as the semester ends. However, the professor refuses to hastily take her virtue. Instead, he wants to slowly teach her the most important lessons of lovemaking.

As she experiences first-time pleasures and passions, love blooms.

By the time they're done, he'll know every inch of her body. But with the pressure building around his show and her sexual debut, will Jem be the one to take her all the way?

About A.C. Rose

A.C. Rose is a sexuality, relationships and health journalist. And she is also an author of steamy romance novels about soulmates who find each other in slightly mystical ways.

She originally wrote *Falling Hard for Fifty* as a final paper for her course "Theories in Love and Romance," while completing a psychology degree. She added to it with interviews she conducted on the topic of *Fifty Shades of Grey* and the new erotic romance phenomenon between 2012 and 2015.

As a former editor of *Playgirl Magazine*, sexy stories and beautiful men have long been her beat. For many years she has written about love, romance, relationships, and sexual health, as well as male and female desires and fantasies.

She specialized in coverage of *Fifty Shades of Grey* when it launched as a worldwide publishing phenomenon and she covered the erotic romance revolution that followed. She is founder of the Fifty Shades of Grey News page on Facebook

She was a reporter for *Romance at Random*, where she regularly interviewed today's most popular steamy romance authors, and now continues that work in her column, *Hot Romance*, on *The Three Tomatoes*.

She is a member of the Romance Writers of America (RWA) and the Author's Guild (AG).

Connect with A. C. Rose here:

Hot Romance Column:
http://thethreetomatoes.com/category/love-sex/hot-romance

Website: http://www.acroseauthor.net/
Blog: http://acroseauthor.com/
Facebook: https://www.facebook.com/AuthorACRose
Fifty Shades of Grey News:
https://www.facebook.com/FiftyShadesOfGreyFans
Twitter: https://twitter.com/ACRoseAuthor
E-mail: acrose@acroseauthor.net

Subscribe to my VIP List.
http://bit.ly/ACRoseList